CONTENTS

The Pricing Strategy Audit

An In-Company Assessment to Help
Create the Best Possible Pricing
Strategy for Your Organization

Kent B. Monroe
The University of Illinois

FINANCIAL TIMES
Prentice Hall

An imprint of **PEARSON EDUCATION**

London • New York • San Francisco • Toronto • Sydney
Tokyo • Singapore • Hong Kong • Cape Town • Madrid • Paris • Milan • Munich • Amsterdam

PEARSON EDUCATION LIMITED

Head Office:
Edinburgh Gate
Harlow CM20 2JE
Tel: +44 (0)1279 623623
Fax: +44 (0)1279 431059

London Office:
128 Long Acre, London WC2E 9AN
Tel: +44 (0)207 447 2000
Fax: +44 (0)207 240 5771
Website: www.business-minds.com

First published in Great Britain in 2000

© Cambridge Strategy Publications Ltd 2000

Published in association with
Cambridge Strategy Publications Ltd
39 Cambridge Place
Cambridge CB2 1NS

The right of Kent B. Monroe to be identified as Author
of this Work has been asserted by him in accordance
with the Copyright, Design and Patents Act 1988.

ISBN 0 273 64938 8

British Library Cataloguing in Publication Data
A CIP catalogue record for this book can be obtained from the British Library

10 9 8 7 6 5 4 3 2 1

Typeset by Pantek Arts, Maidstone, Kent
Printed and bound in Great Britain

The Publishers' policy is to use paper manufactured from sustainable forests.

THE PRICING STRATEGY AUDIT

This audit is structured in three parts. Part 1 examines the process of carrying out a pricing strategy audit. Part 2 looks at the audit process itself and provides a framework that addresses some of the logistical and process requirements of conducting an audit. Part 3 comprises a series of questions based on the six steps in Part 1. These questions are designed to help you plan and implement your audit in a straightforward and practical manner.

INTRODUCTION
TO PRICING

A potential car buyer was interested in purchasing a new full-size automobile. He found just what he was looking for, but its price was more than he felt he could afford—$22,000. He then found a smaller model for $4000 less with the features he wanted. However, he decided to look at some used cars and found a one-year-old full-size model with only 5000 miles on it. The used car included almost a full warranty and was priced at $16,000. He could not overlook the $6000 difference between his first choice and the similar one-year-old car, and decided to purchase the used car.

This simple example illustrates an important aspect of pricing not often recognized: buyers respond to price differences rather than to specific prices. This buyer was responding to a *relatively* lower price, and the *difference* of $6000 eventually led him to buy a used car.

Now consider the automobile maker who has to set the price of new cars. This decision-maker needs to consider how the price will compare: (1) with prices for similar cars by other car makers, (2) with other models in the seller's line of cars, and (3) with used car prices. The car maker also must consider whether the car dealers will be able to make a sufficient profit from selling the car to be motivated to promote it in the local markets. Finally, if the number of new cars sold at the price set is insufficient to reach the profitability goals of the maker, price reductions in the form of cash rebates or special financing arrangements for buyers might have to be used.

Besides these pricing decisions, the car maker must decide on the discount in the price to give to fleet buyers like car rental companies who now account for over 35 percent of all new car sales. Within one year these new rental cars will be sold at special sales to dealers and to individuals like the buyer above. Complicating the pricing of new cars even further is the increasing use of leases. From a buyer's perspective, leasing reduces the size of monthly payments. When buying cars, buyers consider not only the sticker price, but also the amount of down payment and the following monthly payments. Thus, it can be seen that the different types of pricing decisions a seller must make, and the various ways buyers and distributors may react to these prices, makes pricing a very complex, yet strategically important marketing decision.

Pricing is the only marketing strategy variable that directly generates income. All other variables in the marketing mix—advertising, product development, sales promotion, distribution—involve expenditures. Firms often determine prices by marking up cost figures supplied by the financial division and therefore are left primarily with promotion and distribution decisions. However, the pressures of adapting to today's volatile environment in deregulated or emerging marketing economies and enlarging free trade zones has placed additional pressures on pricing decision makers throughout the world.

The Role of Price

In a market economy prices influence *what* products and services should be produced and in what amounts. Prices influence *how* these products and services should be produced. And prices influence *for whom* the products and services should be produced.

Thus, prices affect incomes *and* buying behavior. For the consumer with a given income level, prices influence what to buy and how much of each product to buy. For business firms, profits represent the difference between their revenues and their costs, and their revenues are determined by multiplying price per unit sold by the number of units sold.

Price changes also play a major role in a market economy. When the quantity demanded for a product or service is greater than the supply available, buyers bid up the price. The higher price usually leads to greater profits and an incentive to produce even greater quantities of the product. The producers are able to bid more for raw material resources. In addition, this greater profitability may also stimulate a greater rate of innovation and the development of new technology. On the other hand, if available supply is greater than demand there are pressures to decrease prices and reduce output. These pressures lead producers to convert their resources to alternative uses. Rising prices direct resources to the bidder of greatest desire (stimulating supply) and rising prices curtail demands of the least urgent bidders (rationing supply). Declining prices have the opposite effects.

The Definition of Price

Within this economic context, it is usual to think of price as the amount of money we must give up to acquire something we desire. However, as shown in Figure 1, it is useful to think of price as a ratio of what buyers receive in the way of goods and services relative to what they give up in the way of money or goods and services. In other words, *price is the ratio of what is received relative to what is given up*.

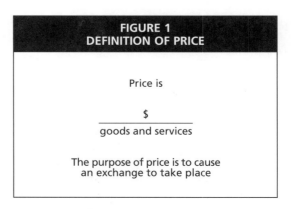

**FIGURE 1
DEFINITION OF PRICE**

Price is

$$\frac{\$}{\text{goods and services}}$$

The purpose of price is to cause an exchange to take place

4

Thus, when the price of a pair of shoes is quoted as $85, the interpretation is the seller receives $85 from the buyer and the buyer receives one pair of shoes. Similarly, the quotation of two shirts for $55 indicates the seller receives $55 and the buyer receives two shirts. Over time a lengthy list of terms have evolved that are used instead of the term 'price'. For example, we pay a postage *rate* to the postal service. *Fees* are paid to doctors and dentists. We pay *premiums* for insurance coverage, *rent* for apartments, *tuition* for education, and *fares* for taxis, buses, and airlines. And we pay *tolls* to cross a bridge, *admission* to go to a sporting event, concert, movie, or museum. Banks may have *user fees* for credit cards, *minimum required balances* for a checking account service, *rents* for safety deposit boxes, and *fees* or *interest charges* for automatic teller machine (ATM) use or cash advances. Moreover, in international marketing *tariffs* and *duties* are paid to import goods into another country.

Suppose the seller wishes to change the price quotation. To illustrate the complexity of pricing, Exhibit 1 illustrates the different ways to change the above ratio. Many organizations pay attention only to the numerator of the ratio (the amount of money to be received) and ignore the denominator. Also, by focusing their attention on the numerator, they encourage their customers to think of price only in monetary terms. Firms taking a value orientation to pricing consider both sides of the ratio.

EXHIBIT 1
SEVEN WAYS TO CHANGE PRICE

Some time ago a shortage of cocoa beans resulted in a shortage of chocolate for candy manufacturers. This shortage of chocolate also resulted in an increase in the price of chocolate. Prior to this shortage, a multipack of six candy bars was priced at $0.89. One candy company changed price by increasing the quantity of money to be given up by the buyer and quoted its candy at $1.19 for six candy bars. Thus, a way to change price is to:
• *change the quantity of money or goods and services to be paid by the buyer.*

However, another candy company changed the price of its multipack by decreasing the number of candy bars in a multipack to five and quoted its candy at $0.89 for five bars. A seller may change the quantity of goods and services by changing the number of items, or the quantity of goods and services may be changed by changing the weight (contents). For example, a box of cereal may be reduced from 16 oz to 14 oz for the same amount of money. Hence, a way to change price is to:
• *change the quantity of goods and services provided by the seller.*

If the quantity ratio remains unchanged, but the quality has been decreased, then the price has increased because the buyer actually receives less. If quality is raised without changing the quantity ratio, then the price has decreased. Thus, a seller can change price by:
• *changing the quality of goods and services provided.*

Suppose a seller quotes a 5 percent discount for all quantity purchases of 100 units or more. If each unit sells for $4, then anyone who purchases 1 to 99 units pays $4 per unit. However, if a customer buys 150 units, then the price is actually $3.80 per unit. Price can also be changed by offering premiums with purchases, such as trading stamps, toys, glasses, or frequent purchase rewards. In each case, if the quantity ratio remains constant, a premium serves to reduce the actual price paid, because the buyer receives additional goods or services. Thus, price can be changed by:

• *changing the premiums or discounts to be applied for quantity variations.*

A practice in the retailing of furniture provides for a complete inventory to be stored at the retail store, thereby allowing the buyer to take immediate possession instead of waiting several months for delivery. These furniture stores generally have three different price tags on the furniture. If buyers wish to pay cash and take the item home, they pay a lower price than buyers who pay cash and have the store deliver it. Buyers who prefer an installment purchase and delivery pay the highest price. These different prices explicitly recognize the differences in selling costs and services, and the furniture store, in effect, transfers the delivery costs to the buyers. Thus, price can be changed by:

• *changing the time and place of transfer of ownership.*

Being able to purchase a product and having 90 days to pay without interest is an actual reduction in price over paying at the time of purchase. Many retail revolving charge accounts provide for no interest charges if the balance is paid within 25 days. Since money has a time value, permitting customers to have the merchandise for a time without paying for it is a reduction in price. In addition, many business firms give discounts for cash payments made at the time of purchase or within a short period after purchase. For example, if payment is received by the tenth of the month, a 2 percent discount may be allowed. Often the actual price is changed if:

• *the place and time of payment are changed.*

Some businesses do not accept checks, other firms operate on a cash-only basis, while others accept credit charges for regular customers. Some gasoline retailers quote a cash price that is lower than the credit price. Thus, another way of changing price is to:

• *change the acceptable form of payment.*

Source: Kent B. Monroe, (1990) *Pricing: Making Profitable Decisions*, New York: McGraw-Hill, pp. 6–7.

Proactive Pricing

The need for correct pricing decisions has become even more important as global competition has become more intense. Technological progress has widened the alternative uses of buyers' money and time and led to more substitute products and services. Organizations successful in making profitable pricing decisions have taken what may be called a proactive pricing approach. They have been able to raise or reduce prices without competitive retaliation. Through careful analysis and deliberate acquisition of pertinent information, they have become successful pricing strategists and tacticians.

There are two essential prerequisites for becoming a successful proactive pricer. First, it is necessary to understand how pricing works. Because of the complexities of pricing in terms of its impact on suppliers, salespeople, distribution, competitors and customers, companies focusing primarily on their internal costs often make serious pricing errors. Secondly, it is essential for any pricer to understand the pricing environment. It is important to know how customers perceive prices and price changes. Often, price is used not only as an indicator of how much money the buyer must give up, but also as an indicator of product or service quality. Moreover, differences between the prices of alternative choices also affect buyers' perceptions. The price setter must know who makes the purchase decision for the products being priced and how this buyer perceives price information.

Factors to Consider When Setting Price

There are five essential factors to consider when setting price. As shown in Figure 2, *demand* considerations provide a ceiling or maximum price to be charged. This maximum price depends on the customers' perceptions of value in the seller's product or service offering. On the other hand, *costs* provide a floor or minimum possible price. For existing products or services, the relevant costs are those costs directly associated with the production, marketing, and distribution of these products or services. For a new product or service, the relevant costs are the *future costs* over the offering's life. The difference between the maximum price some buyers are willing to pay (value) and the minimum cost-based price represents an initial pricing discretion. However, this range of pricing discretion is narrowed by *competition, corporate profit and market objectives* and *regulatory constraints*.

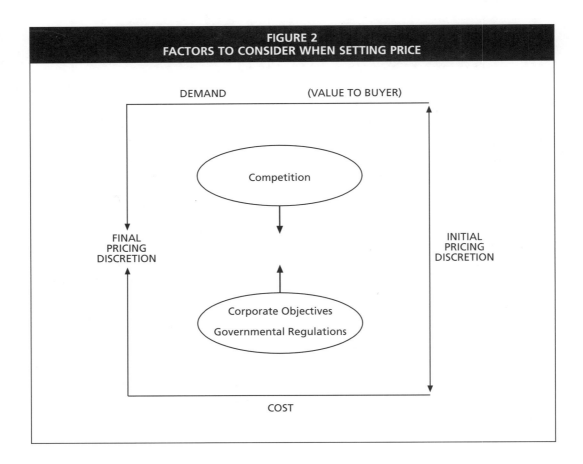

FIGURE 2
FACTORS TO CONSIDER WHEN SETTING PRICE

Summary

1. Setting prices is a complex process that is central to designing a successful marketing mix.

2. In a market economy, prices determine what products and services should be produced, how they should be produced, and for whom.

3. Price differs from other elements of the marketing mix—product, distribution, and promotion—because it does not represent an out-of-pocket cost.

4. Price represents the relationship between what buyers give up in the way of money or goods and services relative to what they gain by acquiring goods and services.

5. Price can be changed in ways other than changing the amount of money to be received for a product or service.

6. The important factors to consider when setting price are demand, cost, corporate objectives, competition, and government regulation.

GUIDELINES FOR DEVELOPING EFFECTIVE PRICING STRATEGIES AND TACTICS

This chapter reviews some of the basic prescriptions for improving the pricing function and presents a set of guidelines for developing and maintaining an effective organizational approach for solving pricing problems. The technical elements of pricing and strategy will be detailed in the rest of the audit.

Setting Up an Audit Team

Often an audit of an organization's pricing strategy and tactics leads to the establishing a pricing management unit or department. Therefore, when setting up the audit team, it is important to use the same process as if the organization was in the process of establishing such a management unit. The audit team ideally should be comprised of about five people who have sufficient knowledge of the firm's offerings and history to be able to understand how the firm has evolved to where it is now. The individuals chosen for the audit team should have skills and knowledge in marketing, should have a working knowledge of finance and be knowledgeable about the firm's products, distribution system and its competitors. The audit team should report to a high level in the organization, should receive sufficient resources to do the audit, and its members should have some prior experience in pricing.

Four Basic Rules for Pricing

The order of the rules does not imply a hierarchy, as each rule is equally important.

Know Your Costs

First, determine the basic cost data necessary for the pricing decision. Know which costs vary directly with changes in levels of activity, and the underlying causes of the changes in costs. Identify costs directly related to the product or service being costed, but not varying with activity levels-direct period or fixed costs. Assign marketing and distribution costs objectively to the products and don't simply lump them into a general overhead category.

Valid cost data provide an objective basis for choosing between pricing alternatives, determining discounts, and establishing differential pricing alternatives. Furthermore, objective cost studies completed before the pricing decisions provide the firm with a valid legal justification for its price structure.

Know Your Demand

You must understand fully the factors influencing the demand for your products and services. Demand analysis is not as objective or as quantifiable as cost analysis, but it is critically important. The key question is the role of price in the purchaser's decision process. Price and price differentials influence buyer perceptions of value.

You also have to know how buyers use the product or service. Is the product used as an input in the buyer's production process? If so, does it represent a significant or insignificant portion of the buyer's manufacturing costs? If the product is a major cost element, small changes in price may significantly affect the buyer's costs and the resulting price of the manufactured product. If the final market is sensitive to price increases, a small price increase to the final manufacturer may significantly reduce demand to the initial seller of the input material.

The seller should also know the different types of distributors and their function in the distribution channel. This is particularly important when the manufacturer sells both to distributors and to the distributors' customers.

Know Your Competition and Your Market

It is important to understand the operations of both domestic and foreign competitors, their rate of capacity utilization, and their products and services. In many markets, the dynamic interaction of supply and demand influences prices. Moreover, changes in capacity availability due to capital investment programs will influence supply and prices. A second important aspect of knowing the market is the need to determine price–volume relationships.

Know Your Objectives

Many firms stress the profit objective of return on investment. Other firms stress the objective of maintaining specified profit margins, while still others seek to achieve market share goals. It is not necessary for each product to maintain the same profit margin in order to achieve a particular return on investment. Similarly, different margins on products may still produce an overall desired corporate profit goal. Finally, firms stressing market share may utilize the experience curve factor and build profits by reducing prices.

Differences in corporate profit objectives will eventually lead to differences in prices and the role of price in influencing actual profits. Thus, imitating or following the pricing practices of other companies is not necessarily in your best interests. Successful pricing is adaptive pricing.

Adaptive Pricing

Adaptive pricing explicitly recognizes the role of costs, corporate goals, and competition, as well as the effect of price and the total interaction of the marketing mix variables on demand when making pricing decisions. Moreover, adaptive pricing provides for a formal mechanism for adapting to environmental changes.

Adaptive pricing provides for the formal use of:

(1) plans and standards of controls

(2) review and analysis of deviations between planned and actual results, and

(3) an information feedback system providing for revision of plans, standards, and policies.

The decision to commit resources involves analyzing a variety of variables that interact with price:

(1) product characteristics

(2) price–product quality relationships

(3) the distribution organization for marketing the products

(4) advertising and other communicative efforts

(5) the quality and nature of services to offer with the products.

The main features of adaptive pricing are:

• demand and the responsiveness of demand to the marketing mix variables are explicitly considered

• the constraining influences of competitive products and services and legal and regulatory forces are recognized

• the necessity to develop a mechanism for adapting to changing market and environmental forces is considered.

Hence, a pricing goal *per se* exists only in the context of an adaptive marketing plan. The adaptive marketing plan should determine investments and cost behavior, rather than existing investments and cost behavior determining pricing and marketing decisions.

Guidelines for Better Pricing Decisions

Set Consistent Objectives

1. Make sure operating objectives are clearly stated, operational, and mutually consistent.

2. When there are several objectives, develop priorities, or otherwise clarify the relationships between the objectives.

3. Make sure everyone concerned with a pricing decision, at any level in the firm, understands the relevant objectives.

4. Translate the operating and financial objectives into buyer and market behavioral objectives.

Identify Alternatives

1. Identify enough alternatives to permit a sensible choice between courses of action.

2. Avoid traditional thinking, encourage creativity.

3. Consider all feasible alternatives regardless of past success or failures.

Acquire Relevant Information

1. Be sure information about buyers, distributors and competitors is current and reflects their current and future situations.

2. Make sure information is for the future, not just a report of the past.

3. Develop a pricing research and information program.

4. Make sure cost information identifies which costs will be affected by a particular pricing alternative.

5. Communicate with and involve accounting people in the cost aspects of a pricing decision.

6. Analyze the effect a particular alternative will have on scarce resources, inventories, production, cashflows, market share, volume, and profits.

7. Be aware of the effects of price changes and price differences on demand and costs.

Make the Pricing Decision

1. Make full use of the information available.

2. Correctly relate all the relevant variables in the problem.

3. Use sensitivity analysis to determine which elements in the decision are most important.

4. Consider all human and organizational problems which could occur with a given pricing decision.

5. Consider the long-term effects of the pricing decision.

6. Base the pricing decision on the lifecycle of each product.

7. Consider the effect of experience in reducing costs as the cumulative production and sales volume increases.

Maintain Feedback and Control

1. Develop procedures to ensure pricing decisions fit into the firm's overall marketing strategy.

2. Provide a feedback mechanism to ensure all who should know the results of the individual price decisions are fully informed.

Summary

To summarize, pricing decisions should be made logically and involve rigorous thinking, with minimum difficulty based on human and organizational factors. They require judgment and predictions about the future, rather than being based on the past. Finally, pricing decisions should be made within the context of a dynamic, long-run corporate and marketing strategy.

Assess the Consistency Between Corporate and Pricing Objectives

An organization's objectives for its pricing strategy should flow from at least two prior levels of planning. First, overall corporate objectives must be considered. Even as broad a goal as being the industry leader will affect pricing objectives. Second, the organization's specific marketing objectives should be based on those corporate objectives. Pricing objectives should be consistent with and advance corporate and marketing objectives. They can be classified according to profitability or financial goals, sales volume, and competitive factors.

Profitability Objectives

Pricing objectives need to be measured precisely. Performance can then be compared with objectives to assess results. *Profitability objectives* may be expressed in specific dollars or as a percentage of sales. For example, a firm may seek average profits of $11 million per year, or a 10 percent increase in total revenues before taxes.

Profit Maximization

In practice, maximum profits may be realized in many different ways. In some markets relatively low prices result in greater sales and higher profits. But in other markets, relatively high prices result in slightly decreased unit sales, and also higher profits. Thus, the profit margins of some firms may be predicated on low prices, high turnover, and high sales volume.

Target Return on Investment

A common pricing objective is some form of *target return on investment* (ROI). This is expressed as the ratio of profits to investments. For manufacturers, investments include capital, machinery, buildings, and land, as well as inventory. For wholesalers and retailers, inventory and buildings constitute the bulk of investments; consequently, an ROI objective is a specific percentage of the revenues above the cost of products purchased for resale.

A variation on ROI objectives is *target return on sales*, whereby the firm sets a profit goal for each unit sold. If a manufacturer sells a product to retailers for $10 per unit, the target profit (return on sales) may be set at $1 per unit.

Volume-Based Objectives

Some organizations set pricing objectives in terms of sales volume. A common goal is sales growth, in which case the firm sets prices to increase demand. Other firms may seek sales maintenance, knowing growth does not ensure higher profits and the organization may not have the resources needed to pursue sales growth.

The Product Mix

An organization's pricing objectives should reflect its strategic orientations. For example, relatively low prices may be set for certain product lines to achieve a faster sales growth than the market in general. Alternatively, a strategy of slower growth for other products may indicate higher prices and profit margins than are common in the market.

Market Share

If capturing a high market share is a marketing objective, pricing objectives should reflect this goal. In general, a high market share is achieved by setting prices relatively low to increase sales. From a profitability perspective, the organization must be willing to accept lower initial profits in exchange for profits produced over time by increased volume and high market share. However, other companies achieve a strong position in selected markets by setting high prices and offering high-quality products and service.

Competitive Objectives

At times, firms base their pricing objectives on competitive strategies. Sometimes the goal is to achieve price stability and engage in non-price competition, while at other times they price aggressively.

Price Stability

When marketing a mature product and when the firm is the market leader, it may seek to stabilize prices. In these circumstances, market leaders can force competitors to follow the market leaders' pricing because stabilization benefits everyone. Price stability often leads to *non-price competition* in which a firm's strategy is advanced by other components of the marketing mix: the product itself, the distribution system or the promotional efforts.

Aggressive Pricing

In some markets, a firm may choose to price aggressively to take advantage of market changes, for example when products are in early stages of the lifecycle, when markets are still growing and when there are opportunities to establish or gain a large market share. As with a market share or volume objective, this aggressiveness must be considered within the context of a longer term perspective.

Summary

By the end of Step 1 the audit team will have:

• set its pricing objectives in terms of profitability, volume and competition

• measured performance against those objectives

• evaluated the consistency of pricing objectives with overall corporate goals.

ASSESS THE RELEVANT ECONOMICS FOR THE PRICING STRATEGY

One of the most important cornerstones of price determination is demand. In particular, the volume of a product buyers are willing to buy at a specific price is the product's demand. The discipline of economics provides some important analytical concepts for practical pricing decisions.

Influence of Price on Buyer Behavior

In economic theory, price influences buyer choice because it serves as an indicator of product or service cost. Assuming the buyer has perfect information concerning prices and wants satisfaction of comparable product alternatives, he or she can determine a product/service mix to maximize satisfaction within a given budget constraint. However, lacking complete and accurate information about the satisfaction associated with the alternative choices, the buyer assesses them on the basis of known information. Generally, one piece of information available to the buyer is a product's price. Other pieces of information about anticipated purchases are not always known and buyers cannot be sure how reliable and how complete this other information is. And because this other information is not always available, buyers may be uncertain about their ability to predict how much they will be satisfied if they purchase the product. For example, if you buy a new car, you do not know what the relative incidence of car repairs will be for the new car until after some months or years of use. *As a result of this imperfect information, buyers may use price as an indicator of product cost as well as an indicator of quality.*

Useful Economic Concepts

This brief outline of how price influences demand does not tell us about the extent to which price and demand are related for each product/service choice, nor does it help us to compare, for example, engineering services per dollar to accounting services per dollar. The concept of elasticity provides a quantitative way of making comparisons across product and service choices.

Demand Elasticity

Price elasticity of demand measures how the quantity demanded for a product or service changes due to an alteration in the price of the product or service. Specifically, price elasticity of demand is defined as the percentage change in quantity demanded relative to the percentage change in price. Normally, it is assumed that quantity demanded falls as price increases.

Since demand elasticity is relative, various goods and services show a range of price sensitivity. *Elastic demand* exists when a given percentage change in price results in a greater percentage change in the quantity demanded. As shown in Figure 3a, a price change from $1000 to $900 increases the quantity demanded from 1000 to 1400 units. Total revenue thus rises from $1 million to $1.26 million. (Because we have not considered what has happened to costs, we cannot assume this increase in revenues means profits have increased.)

When demand is *inelastic*, a given percentage change in price results in a smaller percentage change in the quantity demanded. As Figure 3b shows, a price cut from $1000 to $900 increases the quantity demanded from 1000 units to only 1050 units. Thus, total revenue declines from $1 million to $945,000. A price increase under conditions of inelastic demand would lead to greater total revenue.

Income elasticity of demand is the percentage change in quantity demanded of a product or service relative to a percentage change in personal income. If income elasticity is negative, as income goes up fewer units are demanded. If income elasticity is positive, demand increases as income increases.

A third measure of demand sensitivity is *cross price elasticity of demand*, measuring the responsiveness of demand for a product or service relative to a change in the price

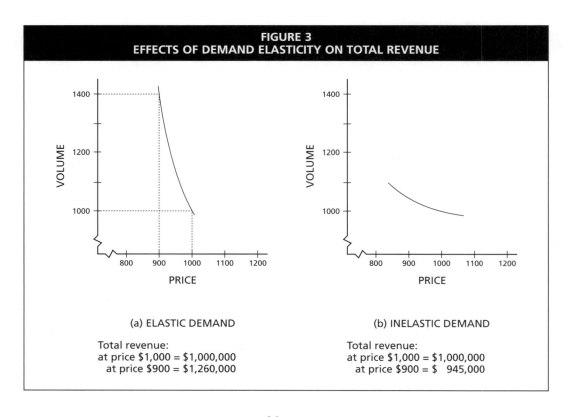

FIGURE 3
EFFECTS OF DEMAND ELASTICITY ON TOTAL REVENUE

(a) ELASTIC DEMAND

Total revenue:
at price $1,000 = $1,000,000
at price $900 = $1,260,000

(b) INELASTIC DEMAND

Total revenue:
at price $1,000 = $1,000,000
at price $900 = $ 945,000

of another product or service. If this relation is negative, in general, the two products are complementary; if the relation is positive, in general, the two products are substitutes.

Products which can be readily substituted for each other are said to have high cross price elasticity of demand. This point applies not only to brands within one product class but also to different product classes. For example, as the price of ice cream goes up (fueled by the rise of super premium brands), consumers may switch to cakes for dessert, thereby increasing the sales of cake mixes.

Razors and razor blades, dress shirts and neckties, and cameras and film are all complementary products. Because such items are typically used together, price changes for one product affect sales of the other. Traditionally, Kodak has priced its camera prices relatively low to increase sales of cameras. Increasing the number of cameras sold increases the demand for film and processing services. Cross price elasticity is often used as a measure of the effects of competitive price changes, and is an important pricing concept.

Revenue Concepts

As we have indicated, there is a relationship between sellers' revenues and the elasticity of demand for their products and services. To establish this relationship we need to define the concepts of total revenue, average revenue, and marginal revenue. *Total revenue* is the total amount spent by buyers for the product (TR = P x Q). *Average revenue* is the total outlay by buyers divided by the number of units sold, or the price of the product (AR = TR÷Q). *Marginal revenue* refers to the change in total revenue resulting from a change in sales volume.

Consumers' Surplus

At any particular price, there are usually some consumers willing to pay more than that price in order to acquire the product. Essentially, this willingness to pay more means the price charged for the product may be lower than some buyers' *perceived value*. The difference between the maximum amount consumers are willing to pay for a product or service and the amount they actually pay is called *consumers' surplus*. In essence, it is the money value of the willingness of consumers to pay in excess of what the price requires them to pay. This difference represents what the consumers gain from the exchange. The difference is the money amounts of *value-in-use* (what is gained) minus *value-in-exchange* (what is given up), and for voluntary exchanges is always positive. Value-in-use always exceeds value-in exchange simply because the most anyone would pay must be greater than what they actually pay otherwise they would not enter into the trade.

For example, assume an orthodontist's fees for a two-year program of corrective treatment is $2400, or $100 per month, and 100 patients subscribe to the service. The aggregate value-in-exchange is $2400 x 100 patients, or $240,000. However, assume each of these patients would have been willing to subscribe to the service for up to $120 per month. That is, the maximum acceptable price is $120 per month, or $2880 over the two years. The total amount these 100 people would have been willing to pay or their value-in-use is $288,000. The difference between the value-in-use and the value-in-exchange, $48,000, is their consumers' surplus.

The important point to grasp is, the price at which exchange takes place is not the equivalent of value, as is so often assumed. Total willingness to pay (value-in-use) is comprised of value-in-exchange and consumers' surplus. This concept of consumers' surplus becomes an important consideration in the determination of prices. Rather than concentrating on cost considerations when setting price, the pricing problem becomes one of determining potential customers' perceived value-in-use, and pricing accordingly.

EXHIBIT 2		
SEARCH, EXPERIENCE AND CREDENCE ATTRIBUTES		

	SEARCH ATTRIBUTES	EXPERIENCE ATTRIBUTES	CREDENCE ATTRIBUTES
Definition	Can be evaluated before purchase	Can be evaluated only after purchase	Usually cannot be evaluated after receipt or use
Examples	Dentist's fees, air travel time, TV picture quality, stereo sound	Food taste, concert performance, dry cleaning, hair perm	Legal advice, tax advice, health care
Therefore, buyers may be . . .	. . . more aware of substitutes	. . . less aware of substitutes	. . . not able to compare or evaluate alternatives
Sellers likely will . . .	. . . imitate/copy successful features	. . . be less able to imitate or copy successful features	. . . be more likely to customize offerings
Therefore there will be . . .	. . . more similar substitutes	. . . fewer and less similar substitutes	. . . fewer and more distinctive substitutes
Cross-price elasticity will be relatively . . .	. . . high	. . . moderate	. . . low

Source: Reprinted by permission from Kent B. Monroe (1990) *Pricing: Making Profitable Decisions*, New York: McGraw-Hill, p. 322

Signals

A firm may want to signal to the marketplace the quality of its product using price, advertising, warranties or other signals.

The managerial issue is how information cues can be used to convey quality information about the product or service to buyers. Specifically, a *signal* is an observable, alterable (by the seller) product, service or firm characteristic which may affect buyers' assessments of product quality. Examples of these signals include the price of the product, the brand or store name, store decorations such as plush carpeting and large expenditures on advertising. For these external cues to serve as signals of quality:

- consumers must be able to discern differences in a product, service or firm characteristic or attribute across sellers

- the quality level of products or services in the market must vary with this characteristic or attribute.

Price sensitivity depends on the number of product alternatives about which the consumer is knowledgeable. The more costly it is to acquire information about alternatives relative to the benefits of having the information, the fewer alternatives consumers will inform themselves about and the more price inelastic will be demand. The number of alternatives about which consumers will be knowledgeable depends on whether the benefits of the product or service can be conveyed by search, experience, or credence attributes (see Exhibit 2).

Demand is likely to be more price elastic for products and services which can be evaluated on the basis of search attributes, than for those which can only be evaluated after receipt of the product or service. Generally, the less consumers are able to evaluate the quality of a product or service before receiving it, the less sensitive they will be to price differences between alternatives. Moreover, under such circumstances, it is more likely for price to be used to infer product or service quality. However, an important question remains: when and under what conditions do buyers associate a positive relationship between product or service quality and various external cues? This will be discussed in the next chapter.

Summary

1. A successful price setter must understand how pricing works and how customers perceive prices and price changes.

2. Buyers may use price as an indicator of product cost as well as an indicator of product quality.

3. Price elasticity changes and is different over time, over products, and differs whether price is increasing or decreasing.

By the end of Step 2 the audit team will have:

• reached an understanding of how pricing works

• realized how buyers use price as an indicator of product cost as well as of quality

• grasped the concept of price elasticity.

DETERMINE HOW YOUR
BUYERS PERCEIVE PRICES

A successful proactive pricer sets price to be consistent with customers' perceived value. To understand how customers form value perceptions, it is important to recognize the role of price. Because of the difficulty of evaluating the quality of products before and even after the product has been acquired, how customers form their perceptions of the product becomes an important consideration when setting prices.

Perception

Perception basically involves a process of categorization. We tend to place new experiences into existing familiar classifications. When buyers are confronted by a price different from what they believe they have previously paid, they must decide whether the difference between the old and new prices is significant to them. If the price difference is perceived to be insignificant, they may classify the two prices as similar and act as they have in the past. In a similar manner, when comparing two alternative products, if the prices of the alternatives are perceived as similar, even though they are not identical, some buyers may perceive the prices as equivalent, and choose on bases other than price. On the other hand, if the price differences are perceived as significant, buyers may classify the products as different, and make their choices on the basis of price.

During this perceptual process buyers make heavy use of information cues or clues. Some of these cues are price cues and influence buyers' judgments of whether the price differences are significant. For example, buyers may use prices as indicators of product or service quality.

Price, Perceived Quality and Perceived Value

Would you buy a package of 25 aspirin that costs only 25 cents? Would you be happy to find this bargain, or would you be suspicious about whether the product is inferior to other brands priced at 12 for 89 cents? In fact, most consumers would be cautious about paying such a low relative price. The price of a product tells us not only how much we must give up (sacrifice) to acquire the product, but because of our imperfect information about how the product may satisfy us, the price helps us assess quality and how much we gain if we acquire the product.

Since buyers generally are not able to assess product quality perfectly (i.e. the ability of the product to satisfy them), the *perceived quality* becomes important. Under

25

certain conditions, the perceived quality in a product is positively related to price. Perceptions of value are directly related to buyers' preferences or choices: the larger a buyer's perception of value, the more likely they are to express a willingness to buy or preference for the product. Perceived value represents a trade-off between buyers' perceptions of quality and sacrifice and is positive when perceptions of quality are greater than the perceptions of sacrifice. Figure 4 illustrates this role of price on buyers' perceptions of product quality, sacrifice, value, and willingness to buy.

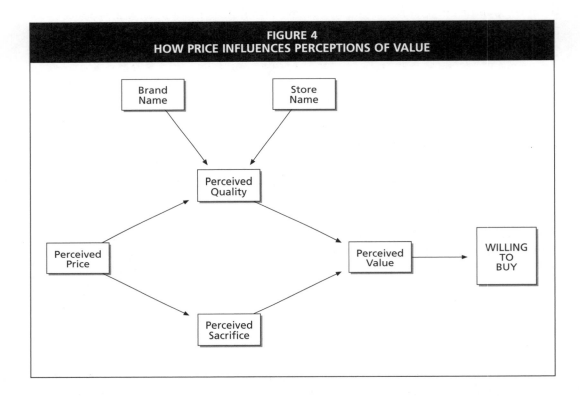

FIGURE 4
HOW PRICE INFLUENCES PERCEPTIONS OF VALUE

The figure also indicates that buyers may use brand name and store name as indicators of product quality (external information cues).

Major Pricing Errors

During the 1990s, companies like General Motors, Apple Computer and PepsiCo began to take a new approach to pricing: 'value pricing'. PepsiCo's Taco Bell chain's sales grew by 15 percent in response to a 'value' menu featuring 59-cent tacos and 14 other items for either 79 cents or 99 cents. While at first glance this may seem to be simply price-cutting, in reality it is more than that. What these companies are doing is attempting to deliver more quality and other product features while holding prices down. For example, Subaru offered its 1991 Loyale sedans equipped with air conditioning, power locks, tinted glass, rear defrosters, and cloth seats for a base price of $9499—just $200 more than the stripped 1990 Loyale. Sales increased about 40 percent in the first six months. Customers' perceptions of value increased even though the price had increased because so much more was being offered relative to the perceived slight increase in price.

Price Thresholds

From psychology we learn that small, equally perceptible changes in a response correspond to proportional changes in the stimulus. For example, if a product's price being raised from $10 to $12 is sufficient to deter you from buying the product, then another product originally priced at $20 would have to be repriced at $24 before you would become similarly disinterested. This general idea provides a basis for discussing the behavioral issues underlying two pricing errors: (1) *not distinguishing between perceived value and price*, and (2) *not distinguishing between absolute price and relative price*.

Absolute price thresholds

Our aspirin example above implies consumers have lower and upper price thresholds: a *range of acceptable prices* for products or services. Furthermore, the existence of a lower price threshold implies some prices are unacceptable because they are considered to be too low, perhaps because buyers are suspicious of the product's quality. Rather than there being a single acceptable price for a product, buyers have some range of acceptable prices. Thus, people may refrain from purchasing a product not only when the price is considered to be too high, but also when the price is considered to be too low.

To illustrate this issue consider the plight of two local accountants who opened a local tax accounting service. They quickly established a reputation of providing excellent service and enjoyed a competitive advantage over the nationally franchised tax consulting services. However, one of the national organizations upgraded its basic service package and offered additional service hours to meet the needs of the local community with a price premium over the local organization. Since the higher price for the service also signaled higher quality, customers perceived a net increase in value. To compete with this change, the local tax accounting service reduced its level of services covered in its basic price in order to maintain a monetary price lower than the national firm. However, customers soon perceived the reduction in the value of the local organization's service, and they shifted their patronage to the national organization. The important lesson to learn from this example is *there are limits or absolute thresholds to the relationship between price and perceived quality and perceived value*. The local tax consulting service failed to recognize this relationship between price and perceived value and reduced its price and perceived value below what customers were willing to pay.

Differential price thresholds

Usually a buyer has alternative choices available for a purchase. However, even if the numerical prices for these alternatives are different, it cannot be assumed the prices are *perceived* to be different. The price setter must determine the effect of perceived *price differences* on buyers' choices. As suggested above, the perception of a price change depends on the magnitude of the change. Indeed, people have been shown to be more sensitive to price increases than decreases.

Generally, it is the perceived relative differences between prices that influence buyers' use of price as an indicator of quality. In a similar way, relative price differences between competing brands, different offerings in a product line, or price levels at different points in time affect buyers' purchase decisions. A recent experience of a major snack food producer illustrates the *error of not recognizing the difference between absolute price and relative price*. At one time, the price of a specific size of this brand's potato chips was $1.39 while a comparable size of the local brand was $1.09. Over time, the price of the national brand increased several times until it was being retailed at $1.69. In like manner, the local brand's price also increased to $1.39. However, while the local brand was maintaining a 30-cent price differential, the national brand obtained a significant gain in market share. The problem was buyers perceived a 30-cent price difference relative to $1.69 as less than a 30-cent price difference relative to $1.39. This example illustrates the notion of *differential price thresholds*, or the degree of buyers' sensitivity to relative price differences.

From behavioral price research, a number of important points about price elasticity have emerged:

- Buyers, in general, are more sensitive to perceived price increases than to perceived price decreases. In practical terms, this difference in relative price elasticity between price increases versus price decreases means it is easier to lose sales by increasing price than it is to gain sales by reducing price.

- Sometimes a product may provide a *unique benefit* or have a *unique attribute* which buyers value. These unique benefits or attributes serve to make the product less price sensitive.

- The *frequency of past price changes* can influence buyers' sensitivity to price changes. If prices have been changing relatively frequently, buyers may not have adjusted to the previous price change when a new change occurs. If buyers have not adjusted to the last price increase, then another price increase will be perceived as a larger increase than it actually is, making them more sensitive to the increase.

Effects of reference prices on perceived value

Price will not serve as a signal of product quality unless there is a perceptible difference in price from the buyer's reference price. Buyers may use as a reference point the range of prices last paid, the current market price or perceived average market price, a belief about a fair price to pay, or an expected price to pay to judge actual prices.

To judge whether a price is acceptable, too high, or too low, it has to be compared to another price. This other comparative price is the buyer's reference price for the particular judgment. Not recognizing this key important point has led to a third pricing error: *not distinguishing between pricing strategies and pricing tactics.*

Price perceptions are relative: a specific price is compared to another price, or a reference price. The illustration for relating this important point to pricing strategy and tactics comes from a firm introducing a new product with an introductory low price. Initially, the product was targeted to sell at a price of $17.50. However, the firm used the tactic of introducing it at a low price of $14.95. Later, when it was time to remove the introduction price, because of increased costs, the regular price was set at $20.00. The product failed to sustain sufficient sales volume to warrant its continued existence. The error in this situation was the pricing tactic of a low introductory price established a baseline or reference price of $14.95 rather than $17.50. Hence, the $20.00 price, when compared to $14.95, was perceived to be too expensive and buyers stopped buying.

Price and Perceived Value

Consumers' perceptions of a price derive from their interpretations of the price differences (real or implied) *and* from their interpretations of the cues in the offer. They make their purchase decisions in a two-step process. First, they *judge* the value of an offer, and then they *decide* whether to make the purchase. Of concern here is how they use price information to judge the value of the offer, and the influence this evaluation has on their purchase decisions.

For example, when sellers advertise both the sale price and a (higher) comparative (regular) price, they are attempting to impose a reference price for consumers' comparisons. To help consumers accept the higher price as a reference price, the sellers may include such words as 'formerly', 'regularly', 'usually' to describe the higher price. Words can be used in a variety of ways to enhance consumers' perceptions of a sale taking place and how the offer represents a saving. Since prices are evaluated comparatively, the judgment of acceptability depends not only on consumers' price expectations, but also on information provided in promotions or advertisements. The perception of savings conveyed by price advertising leads to positive or favorable behavioral responses.

Summary

1. The essence of pricing is determining potential buyers' perceptions of value for products and services.

2. Buyers' perceptions of value represent a comparison between the quality (or benefits) they perceive in the product relative to the cost of acquiring the product.

3. Prices should be set so as to reflect customers' perceptions of value.

4. Buyers determine whether a price is acceptable to pay by comparing it to a reference price.

By the end of Step 3 the audit team will have:

• considered how its customers perceive prices

• evaluated what its prices communicate about its products' quality and value

• distinguished between perceived value and price

• recognized the difference between absolute and relative prices.

DETERMINE THE
RELEVANT COSTS FOR
THE PRICING STRATEGY

Cost data are helpful for deciding what price to set. By determining the difference between costs and the price under consideration and then balancing that margin against the estimated sales volume, the seller can determine whether the product or service will contribute sufficient money to enable the firm to recover its initial investment. When considering the cost aspect of a pricing decision, a crucial question is what costs are relevant to the decision.

It is important for the seller to know the causes and behavior of product costs in order to know when to accelerate cost recovery, how to evaluate a change in selling price, how to segment a market profitably and when to add or eliminate products. Even so, costs play a limited part in pricing. They indicate whether the product or service can be provided and sold profitably at any price, but they do not indicate how much markup or markdown on cost buyers will accept.

Costs for pricing must deal with the future. Current or past information probably will not provide an adequate basis for profit projections. Product costs must be based on expected purchase costs of materials, labor wage rates, and other expenses to be incurred. In addition, information is needed about product development, advertising and promotion, and distribution costs. Planned costs are important, not past costs, since profit planning necessarily deals with the future.

Cost Concepts

To determine profit at any volume, price level, product mix, or time, proper cost classification is required. Some costs vary directly with the rate of activity, while others do not. If the cost data are classified into their fixed and variable components and properly attributed to the activity causing the cost, the effect of volume becomes apparent and sources of profit are revealed. Exhibit 3 defines the cost concepts of importance to pricing.

EXHIBIT 3
CLASSIFYING COSTS

By Activity:

- *Direct costs* (also called *traceable* or *attributable* costs) are those costs incurred solely for a particular product, service, department, program, or customer account. These costs may be fixed or variable. For example, material and labor costs may be traceable to a unit of service provided.

- *Indirect traceable costs* can be traced to a product, service, department, program, or customer account if the costs can be identified with that unit. These costs, although not incurred solely for a product, can be objectively identified with the product. They may be fixed or variable. The time of an agent who serves several clients can be traced to or identified by the amount of time spent on each client's account.

- *Common costs* support a number of activities or profit segments. These costs cannot be traced to a product based on a direct physical relationship to the product. The administration costs of a service facility are common to all units of service provided in the facility. A common or general cost does not change when one of the activities it supports is discontinued. Hence, discontinuing a product in the line will not affect the administration costs of the facility, nor of other general expenses such as market research or research and development.

By Behavior:

- *Direct variable costs* vary directly with an activity level. As production activity is increased in a given period a proportionately higher amount of labor and materials is used. As the production volume is increased these direct variable costs will be constant per additional unit of product or service provided. The main criterion of a direct variable cost is its generation by, and identification with, the providing and delivery of a specific product or service.

- *Semivariable costs* vary with activity rates but are not zero at a zero activity rate. Data processing costs are a good example. The costs of acquiring computer hardware and software are fixed, but the processing costs may vary with the amount of online time used. Hence these semivariable costs consist of a base amount which is constant in relation to activity and a variable amount which varies directly with changes in the activity level.

- *Fixed costs* do not vary with volume. Instead, they remain fixed over a period of time and do not increase as the quantity of services provided increases. Many costs for service organizations are fixed, ranging up to 80 percent of total cost. This means volume shifts can have dramatic implications for the profits of a service organization.

In addition to classifying costs according to ability to attribute a cost to a product or service, it is also important to classify costs according to variation with the rate of activity. As noted above, unless costs can be segmented into fixed and variable, it is not possible to trace the effects of changes in price, volume, or product selling mix.

Some costs vary directly with the activity level, while others, although fixed, are directly attributable to the activity level. Hence, it is important to clarify specifically what is meant by the terms *direct and indirect*. Directly traceable or attributable costs can readily be determined as contributing to the product or service's cost. However, whether a direct cost is variable, fixed, or semivariable depends on properly determining the cause of the cost. Perhaps, more than anything else, managers need to understand how costs are incurred and how they behave as activity levels change.

Break-Even Analysis

Price setters use *break-even analysis* to calculate what quantity of product the firm needs to sell just to cover all costs: the firm suffers no loss but makes no profit, it 'breaks even.'

Break-even analysis requires price setters to know their fixed and variable costs. *Fixed costs* include such expenditures as managers' salaries, building maintenance, insurance, mortgage payments or rent, and debt service—costs remaining constant for a period (usually one or more years), regardless of the level of sales volume or other activities. *Variable costs*, however, include such expenses as hourly wages, raw materials, transportation and shipping, and commissions paid to sales representatives—all of which change as production and sales volume changes (activity levels).

Break-even calculations can be illustrated by a simple formula or a graph. For a single product or service, the formula is:

$$\text{Break-even (in units)} \ = \ \frac{\text{fixed costs}}{(\text{price} - \text{unit variable costs})}$$

The quantity (price – unit variable costs) is referred to as contribution to profit per unit sold. If a firm sells its product to retailers for $40 each, if its fixed costs are $600,000 and its variable costs per unit are $20, the break-even point using the equation presented above is:

$$\text{Break-even} \ = \ \frac{\$600,000}{\$40 - \$20}$$

$$= \ \frac{\$600,000}{\$20}$$

$$= \ 30,000 \text{ units}$$

This firm must sell 30,000 units to break even. If it sells fewer units, it loses money; if it sells more, it makes a profit. Note that it must sell 30,000 units to reach the break-even point at which revenues ($1,200,000) exactly equal total costs ($1,200,000).

Profit Analysis

Virtually every planned action or decision in an organization affects costs, and therefore profits. Profit analysis attempts to determine the effect of costs, prices, and volume on profits in order to determine the best strategy to follow. Knowing the relative profit contributions of each product gives management a sound basis for managing its product lines.

One of the most important pieces of data resulting from a profit analysis is the *contribution ratio*, usually referred to as the *profit–volume ratio* (PV). The PV ratio is the percentage of sales dollars available to cover fixed costs and profits after deducting variable costs. The formula for computing it is:

$$\frac{(price - variable\ cost)}{price}$$

or

$$\frac{\$\ contribution\ per\ unit}{price}$$

For the example above, the contribution ratio or PV is the contribution of $20 divided by price, $40, or 50 percent. Thus, 50 cents out of each sales dollar contribute towards paying fixed costs and then providing a profit.

This PV ratio is an important piece of information for analyzing the profit impact of changes in sales volume, changes in the cost structure of the firm (i.e. the relative amount of fixed costs to total costs), as well as changes in price. For example, if sales initially were $2 million (50,000 units sold), then profit contribution is $1,000,000 ($20 contribution x 50,000) and net profits are $400,000 ($1,000,000 – 600,000). Now, if $100,000 of additional sales are generated, the *additional profits* would be $100,000 x 0.50, or $50,000. Since the fixed costs of $600,000 have already been covered by the original $2 million of sales, additional volume contributes 50 cents of every sales dollar to profits. Thus, a 5 percent increase in sales produces a 12.5 percent increase in profits. This analysis is possible only when all direct and indirect traceable costs have been separated into their fixed and variable components.

Profit Analysis for Multiple Products

As this discussion indicates, for a single product situation, the elements of profitability the firm must consider are: price per unit, sales volume per period, valuable costs per unit, and the direct and objectively assignable fixed costs per period. Extending the break-even analysis to consider the effects of contribution margin (price – unit variable costs) relative to price, the PV ratio, allows us to determine how the changes noted above affect the profitability of a single product. However, it is typical for firms to sell multiple products or offer multiple services, and the cost classification requirements above become more difficult.

In multiproduct firms it is important to put emphasis on achieving the maximum amount of contribution revenue for each product instead of attempting to maximize sales revenues. Each product offering faces different competition, has a different demand elasticity, and perhaps depends for its sales, at least in part, on the sales of the other products in the line. Within a multiproduct firm, each offering generates a different amount of volume, a different cost structure, including variable and fixed costs, different unit prices and, of course, different revenues. Not only are these important factors different, but they are changing.

The PV ratio can be used to analyze the relative profit contributions of each product in the line. Each product has a different PV value and different expected dollar sales volume as a percentage of the line's total dollar volume. In multiproduct situations, the PV is determined by weighting the PV of each product by the percentage of the total dollar volume for all products in the line. For example, assume the firm offers three products, A, B and C. Product A generates 40 percent of the line's dollar revenues, while B and C generate 30 percent each. To determine the overall profit margin for the line, we need to develop a weighted, or composite, PV ratio for the line. This composite is the sum of the weighted PV ratios: $[0.40 \times .40 + 0.20 \times .30 + 0.10 \times 0.30 = 0.25]$.

What happens if the dollar volume mix of the three products changes? To illustrate, assume the PV ratios of the three products remain the same, i.e. *prices and costs do not change*. Product A now contributes 20 percent of the line's dollar revenues, while product B generates 50 percent of the dollar volume and product C continues to generate 30 percent. The composite PV ratio for the line now is $[0.40 \times .20 + 0.20 \times .50 + 0.10 \times 0.30 = 0.21]$. On average, each dollar of revenue generated by sales of products in this line contributes 4 cents less than in the original example. Unless there is a substantial increase in total dollar sales for the line, the firm will earn less profits with this shift in the dollar sales mix.

This potential reduction in profits occurred despite no changes in prices or costs! What did change is the relative way the different products sold in the different markets. For example, stronger competitive activity aimed at product A might have reduced its sales. Or consumers' tastes, and therefore demand, might have shifted towards B, maybe because it is a newer product now entering its sales growth phase. Or it is possible the firm's salespeople were instructed to emphasize the sales of B, which they did quite well to the detriment of sales for A.

Summary

1. It is important for sellers to know the causes and behavior of costs in order to know how to manage the relative profitability of their offerings.

2. Costs for pricing must deal with the future.

3. Profits at any sales level are a function of prices, volume, costs and the product sales mix.

By the end of Step 4 the audit team will have:

• discussed the causes and behavior of product costs

• understood what determines profit

• classified costs by activity and behavior

• carried out break-even analyses

• undertaken a profit analysis in order to ascertain the effects of costs, prices and volume on profits.

DETERMINE THE CHARACTERISTICS OF EACH SPECIFIC PRICE DECISION

As shown in Exhibit 4, a firm must make many kinds of pricing decisions. There is the decision on what specific price to charge for each product and service marketed. But the specific price to charge depends on the type of customer to whom the product is sold. For example, if different customers purchase in varying quantities, should the seller offer volume discounts?

The firm must also decide whether to offer discounts for early payment, and if so, when a customer is eligible for a cash discount and how much to allow for early payment. Should the firm attempt to suggest retail or resale prices or should it only set prices for its immediate customers? When a firm uses other business firms as intermediaries between itself and its customers, it does not have direct contact with its ultimate customers. Yet the way customers respond to prices depends on how they perceive the prices and the relationships between them.

Normally, the firm sells multiple products and these questions must be answered for each product or service offered. Additionally, the need to determine the number of price offerings per type of product and the price relationships between the products offered make the pricing problem more complex. For example, when a manufacturer makes several models of cars and sells to different types of customers, e.g. individuals and fleet car buyers, the seller has made a decision to sell to different market segments. Different types of market segments respond differently to prices, price differences, and price changes.

The firm must also decide whether it will charge customers for the transportation costs incurred when shipping the products to them. Customers located at different distances from the manufacturer will pay a different total price if they are charged for the transportation costs. Yet if the seller quotes a uniform price including the transportation costs regardless of distance from the manufacturer, some buyers may receive the products at a total price less than the costs incurred to the manufacturer, while other customers will pay a price exceeding the total costs incurred by the manufacturer. Such differences in prices to similar types of customers may lead to some concerns about the legality of the pricing policy.

1. What to charge for the different products and services marketed by the firm.

2. What to charge different types of customers.

3. Whether to charge different types of distributors the same price.

4. Whether to give discounts for cash and how quickly payment should be required to earn them.

5. Whether to suggest resale prices or only set prices charged to one's own customers.

6. Whether to price all items in the product line as if they were separate or to price them as a 'team'

7. How many different price offerings to have of one item

8. Whether to base prices on the geographical location of buyers (i.e. whether to charge for transportation)

Source: Kent B. Monroe (1990) *Pricing: Making Profitable Decisions*, New York: McGraw-Hill, p. 278.

Pricing New Products

Determining the price of a new product or service is a decision usually made with very little information on demand, costs, competition, and other variables. Many new products fail because they do not possess the features desired by buyers, or because they are not available at the right time and place. Others fail because they have been wrongly priced, and the error can as easily be in pricing too low as in pricing too high.

Factors to Consider When Pricing New Products

The core of new product pricing takes into account the price sensitivity of demand and the seller's incremental promotional and production costs. What the product is worth to the buyer, not what it costs the seller, is the controlling consideration. What is important when developing a new product's price is the relationship between the buyers' perceived benefits in the new product relative to the total acquisition cost (i.e. financial value), relative to alternative offerings available.

Buyers' Alternatives

The prospective buyer of any new product does have alternatives. These indirectly competitive products or services provide the reference point for appraising the price–performance package of a new product or service, and determine its relative attractiveness to potential buyers. Such an analysis of demand can be made by the following steps:

1. Determine the main uses for the new product. For each application, determine how well the product performs.

2. For each main use, specify the buyers' best alternatives to the new product. Determine the performance characteristics and requirements which buyers view as crucial in determining their selection. Exhibit 5 illustrates some price, quality and value-added performance characteristics.

3. For each main use, determine how well the product's performance characteristics meet the requirements of customers compared with the performance of the alternatives.

4. Forecast the prices of alternative choices in terms of *transaction prices* (the net price after all discounts have been applied). Estimate from the prices of these reference substitutes the alternative costs to the buyer per unit of the new product.

5. Estimate the *superiority premium*, i.e. price the performance differential in terms of what the superior performance provided by the new product is worth to buyers of various categories.

6. Calculate a 'parity price' for the product or service relative to the buyer's best alternative choice in each use, and do this for the main categories of customers. Parity is a price encompassing the premium a customer would be willing to pay for comparative superiority in performance characteristics. What matters is *superiority as buyers value it, not superiority as measured by technicians' measurements or by the seller's costs*.

	EXHIBIT 5		
	CONSUMER DEFINITIONS OF PRICE, QUALITY AND VALUE		
CATEGORY	**PRICE ELEMENTS**	**QUALITY ELEMENTS**	**VALUE ELEMENTS**
Auto parts store	low price; sales; private labels	knowledgeable sales-people; parts in stock	variety of parts; fast service
Bank	service charges; interest rates	financial stability; interest in customers	variety of services; easy-to-understand services
Building product	low cost	easy to work with; durable	easy to install
Coffee shop	low prices; specials	cleanliness; taste of food	hours open; take-out items
Convenience store	reasonable prices	clean interior	variety; easy-to-find items
Discount store	sales/clearances; low prices	selection; well-known brands	easy return; check cashing
Family steak house	low prices; coupons	taste of steak; atmosphere	salad bar; things for children
Furniture store	credit policies; low prices; price ranges	well-known brands; knowledgeable sales-people	delivery; display methods
Gas station	low prices	octane rating; no alcohol in gas; speed of pumps	windshield cleaning
Ice cream	low prices; specials; coupons	taste; richness; flavor; creaminess	container size
Jewelry store	sales; low prices; low interest rates	unique jewelry; custom designing	personal interest in customers; fast service
Pizza restaurant	specials; coupons; promotions; low prices	hot product; taste; consistent product	fast delivery; home delivery; variety

There are two broad alternatives when pricing a new product: 'skimming' pricing calling for a relatively high price, and 'penetration' pricing calling for a relatively low price.

Skimming pricing

Some products represent drastic improvements on accepted ways of performing a function or filling a demand. For these products, a strategy of high prices with large promotional expenditures during market introduction (and lower prices at later stages) may be appropriate when:

1. Sales of the product are likely to be less sensitive to price in the early stages than when it is 'full grown' and competitive imitations have appeared.

2. Launching a new product with a high price is an efficient device for breaking the market up into segments with different price elasticities of demand. The initial high price serves to 'skim the cream' of the market which is relatively insensitive to price.

3. A skimming policy is safer: facing unknown elasticity of demand, a high initial price serves as a 'refusal' price during the exploration stage.

4. High prices may produce greater dollar sales volume during market development than are produced by low initial prices (if the market segment is relatively insensitive to price). If so, skimming pricing will provide funds to finance expansion into the larger-volume sectors of a market.

5. A capacity constraint exists. Demand is likely to be greater than the firm's initial capability to supply this level of demand.

6. There is realistic perceived value in the product on the part of the potential buyers.

Skimming is not always appropriate in these situations and it does have drawbacks. A skimming strategy is less likely to induce buyers into the market and it does not encourage rapid adoption or diffusion of the product. Moreover, if skimming results in relatively high profit margins, competitors may be attracted into the market.

Penetration pricing

A skimming price policy is not appropriate for all new products or services. Using low prices as a wedge to get into mass markets early may be appropriate when:

1. Potential buyers of the product are very sensitive to price, even in the early stages of introduction.

2. It is possible to achieve substantial reductions in unit costs by producing and selling at large volumes.

3. The new product faces threats of strong potential competition soon after introduction.

4. There is no segment of buyers willing to pay a higher price to obtain the product.

A penetration strategy encourages both rapid adoption and diffusion of new products. An innovative firm may thus be able to capture a large market share before its competitors can respond. However, low prices and low profit margins must be offset by high sales volumes. It may be some time before enough profits accrue to recover the costs of product development, production, distribution, and promotion.

To avoid the disadvantages of skimming and penetration, some firms employ both alternatives. They pursue a skimming strategy after a product is first introduced—typically, until competitors enter the market. Then they switch to a penetration strategy by lowering prices to build market share and volume.

One important consideration in the choice between skimming and penetration pricing at the time a new product is introduced is the ease and speed with which competitors can bring out substitute offerings. If the initial price is set low enough, large competitors may not feel it worthwhile to make a big investment for slim profit margins.

Pricing During Growth

If the new product survives the introductory period, as demand grows a number of competitors are usually producing and selling a similar product, and an average market price begins to emerge. Normally, there is a relatively wide range of market prices early in the growth stage, but this market price range narrows as the product approaches maturity.

When pricing products during the growth stage three essential points should be noted: (1) the range of feasible prices has narrowed since the introductory stage, (2) unit variable costs may have decreased due to the experience factor, and (3) fixed expenses have increased because of increased capitalization and period marketing costs. The pricing decision during the growth stage is to select a price which, subject to competitive conditions, will help generate a sales dollar volume enabling the firm to realize its target profit contribution.

Pricing During Maturity

As a product moves into the maturity and saturation stages, it is necessary to review past pricing decisions and determine the desirability of a price change. Replacement sales now constitute the main demand, and manufacturers may also incur competition from retailer-owned brands. Market conditions do not appear to warrant a price increase, hence the pricing decision is usually to reduce price or maintain the current level.

When is a price reduction profitable? We know that when demand is price elastic it is profitable to reduce prices if costs do not rise above the increase in revenues. But since it can be expected that any price decrease will be followed by competitors, it is also necessary that the *market demand* curve be elastic within the range of the price reduction. Moreover, the requirements for a profitable price reduction strategy include beginning with a relative high contribution margin (i.e. relatively high PV ratio), opportunity for accelerating sales growth, and a price elastic demand. When a product has reached the maturity stage of its lifecycle, it is most likely that these conditions will not exist.

Pricing a Declining Product

During the declining phase of a product's life, direct costs are very important to the pricing decision. Normally, competition has driven the price down close to direct costs. Only those sellers who were able to maintain or reduce direct costs during the maturity stage are likely to have remained. If the decline is not due to an overall cyclical decline in business but to shifts in buyer preferences, then the primary objective is to obtain as much contribution to profits as possible.

So long as the firm has excess capacity and revenues exceed all direct costs, it probably should consider remaining in the market. Generally, most firms eliminate all period marketing costs (or as many of these costs as possible) and remain in the market as long as price exceeds direct variable costs. In fact, it might be beneficial to raise the price of a declining product to increase the contribution per sales dollar. In one case, a firm raised the price of an old product to increase contribution while phasing it out of the product line. To its surprise, sales actually grew. There was a small, but profitable market segment for the product after all!

Focused Price Reductions

The stringent requirements for price reduction strategies to be profitable make it questionable ever to consider across-the-board price cuts. Yet, over the product lifecycle, there often is a need to consider reducing prices, either because of competitive pressures, or because there are price-sensitive buyers in the market. Thus, if the firm can selectively reduce price to specific market segments, focused price reductions may be profitable. Information from conducting pricing research and marketing cost analyses must be available to develop a focused price reduction strategy. Some different ways in which focused price reductions can be implemented are offered below.

Base Product versus Option Prices

Often, by selling the basic product without a multitude of add-on features and options, the seller can appeal to a price-sensitive market, those who want only the basic product and to other buyers who are not price sensitive. Many customers will make their purchase decision using the base price alone, and then become less price sensitive to the additional options or accessories purchased separately. Some examples of this include bank practices of separating interest rates and fees, movie theaters separating seat tickets from concessions, automobile buying, and service contracts on consumer appliances.

Channel-Specific Pricing

High-price designer clothing can frequently be purchased in off-price retailers and factory outlets at a fraction of the price in upscale stores. While there may be some differences in the assortment available and in amenities and services provided, fashion clothing can be purchased at relatively lower prices in the former stores. The objective of using this strategy is to identify distribution channels serving price-sensitive customers and offer lower-priced products through these channels only.

Vary Prices According to Customers' Perceived Values

Offering lower prices for demand occurring during off-peak hours, for example long-distance telephone, midnight to 5 am utility rates, is a price-reduction strategy which not only shifts demand, but enhances volume from price-sensitive segments.

Product Redesign

This strategy is a variation of unbundling the base product from the options mentioned above. The difference is the product is changed in some way (fewer features, lower-grade material, different brand name) and sold as a separate, lower-priced product. Again, the objective is to appeal to price-sensitive customers who would normally not buy the original product at its regular price.

Price Bundling

Price bundling is the practice of offering two or more products or services at a price usually less than the sum of the individual prices. It has become a pervasive practice, and like any price-reduction strategy is limited as to when it can be used successfully.

Summary

1. The business firm has many different types of pricing decisions to make in addition to setting the basic or list price.

2. New product pricing decisions are challenging because the decision maker usually has very little information on demand, costs, competition and other variables affecting the chances of success.

3. Pricing strategies for new products generally aim either to 'skim' or to 'penetrate' the market. A skimming strategy usually results in relatively high prices, while a penetration strategy tends to establish relatively low prices.

4. When a product reaches its maturity stage, the most appropriate pricing strategy should attempt to maximize short-run contribution to profits.

By the end of Step 5 the audit team will have:

- made certain fundamental pricing decisions, relating, for example, to differential pricing, discounts and distribution

- considered how new products should be priced

- determined the lifecycle stage for each of its products and therefore the most appropriate pricing strategy.

INTEGRATE SPECIFIC PRICE DECISIONS INTO AN OVERALL PRICING STRATEGY

Generally, a business organization has several lines, each a set of products closely related because they are acquired together, they satisfy the same general needs or they are marketed together. Often some of these products are substitutes for each other, for example different types of checking accounts, different types of savings accounts, or different types of cameras. Other products or services complement each other, for example a financial consultant who offers both tax advice and preparation services as well as investment advice. Because of the demand and cost inter-relationships inherent within a multiple product firm, and because there are usually several price market segments, pricing multiple products is one of the main challenges facing a pricing manager.

Although an organization may wish to pursue a pricing strategy of high prices only (or low prices only), it still must decide how high (or low) its prices should be and the price differentials between different products in the line. In addition, it must decide on the lowest (or highest) price helping to maintain a consistent price policy. Thus, three types of pricing decisions are required:

1. Determining the lowest-priced product and its price (low-end product).

2. Determining the highest-priced product and its price (high-end product).

3. Setting the price differentials for all intermediate products.

The low-end price is usually the most frequently remembered and probably has considerable influence on the marginal buyer (the buyer doubtful about buying, but still seriously considering making the purchase). Hence, the lowest-priced product is often used as a traffic builder. On the other hand, the highest-priced product is also quite visible and, through quality connotations, may also stimulate demand.

Price Bundling

A price bundle can be as simple as pricing a restaurant menu to have both a set dinner or the items *à la carte*, or as complex as offering a ski package including travel, lodging, lift and ski rentals, as well as lessons. In either situation, some important principles need to be considered when bundling products at a special price.

Rationale for Price Bundling

Many businesses are characterized by a relatively high ratio of fixed to variable costs. Moreover, several products or services can usually be offered using the same facilities, equipment and personnel. Thus, the direct variable cost of a particular product or service is usually quite low, meaning the product or service has a relatively high profit–volume (PV) ratio. Thus, the incremental costs of selling additional units are generally low relative to the firm's total costs.

In addition, many of the products or services offered by most organizations are interdependent in terms of demand, either being substitutes for each other or complementing the sales of another offering. Thus, it is appropriate to think in terms of *relationship pricing*, or pricing in terms of the inherent demand relationships among the products or services. The objective of price bundling is to *stimulate demand for the firm's product line to achieve cost economies for the operations as a whole, while increasing net contributions to profits.*

Mixed Bundling

In *mixed bundling*, the customer can purchase products or services individually or as a package. Normally, there is a price incentive to purchase the package. In *mixed-leader bundling* the price of one product is discounted (the lead product) if the first product is purchased at full price. For example, if cable TV customers buy the first premium channel at full price, they may be able to acquire a second premium channel at a reduction from its monthly rate. Assuming premium channels A and B are individually priced at $10 per month each, then B might be offered for $7.50 if A is acquired at its regular rate. In *mixed-joint bundling* there is a single price for the combined set of services. In this situation, the two premium channels would be offered as a set for one price, for example $17.50 per month. As should be obvious from these two examples, the net outlay for the customer buying either bundle is the same, but there is a difference in deciding which bundle to offer.

Since the objective is to increase the overall sales level of the firm, the products selected for bundling should be relatively small in unbundled sales volume. The reason for this prescription is to minimize the cannibalization effects. For mixed-leader bundling, the lead product must be price elastic, have attributes easy to evaluate before purchase, be the higher-volume product in the bundle and the lower-margin product. The objective is to use a price reduction in this product or service to generate an increase in its volume to "pull" an increase in demand for a product with a lower volume, but higher contribution margin. The increase in volume of the second product will contribute more to profits than the loss due to the reduced contribution of the lead product.

For mixed-joint bundling, the contribution margin for each product should be about equal, the unbundles sales volumes should be about equal, their demand should be price elastic and each should complement the other product. In any case, these products should not have high sales volumes.

Yield Management

Another form of segmentation pricing developed by the airlines is yield management. This operates on the principle of different segments of the market for airline travel having different degrees of price sensitivity. Therefore, seats on flights are priced differently depending on the time of day, day of the week, length of stay in the destination city before return, when the ticket is purchased, and a willingness to accept certain conditions or restrictions on when to travel. Besides the airlines, hotels, telephone companies, rental car companies, banks and savings and loans have used yield management to increase sales revenues through segmentation pricing. Retail firms are likely to be able to use yield management to determine when to mark down slow-moving merchandise and when to schedule sales.

The unique benefit of the yield management pricing program lies in forcing management continuously to monitor demand for its products. Further, changes in demand lead to pricing changes in response. If the product is not selling fast enough, price reductions can be initiated to stimulate sales. With relatively high contribution margins (high PV ratios), small price reductions do not require large increases in volume to be profitable.

Summary

1. When pricing a product line, there are three basic pricing decisions:
   - determining the lowest-priced product and its price
   - determining the highest-priced product and its price, and
   - setting the price differentials for all intermediate products in the line.

2. The objective of price bundling as a form of product-line pricing is to stimulate demand for a firm's products to achieve cost economies.

3. In general, the products selected for price bundling should be relatively small in unbundled sales in order to minimize cannibalization.

4. Yield management pricing as practiced by the airlines is a form of segmented pricing.

By the end of Step 6 the audit team will have:

- determined the lowest-priced product and its price

• determined the highest-priced product and its price

• set the price differentials for all intermediate products

• considered whether some products can be bundled as a package

• decided whether yield management pricing is applicable.

ASSESS THE ADMINISTRATIVE STRUCTURE FOR MANAGING THE PRICING FUNCTION

Perhaps the most difficult aspect of the pricing decision is developing procedures and policies for administering prices. Up to this point, the issue has been setting base or list prices. However, the list price is rarely the actual price paid by the buyer. The price actually paid is changed by a decision to discount from list price for volume purchases or early payment, to extend credit, or to charge for transportation.

Pricing decisions and their implementation can have an effect on dealer or distributor cooperation and motivation as well as on salespeople's morale and effort. While it is difficult to control prices legally through the distribution channel, it is possible to elicit cooperation and provide motivation to adhere to company-determined pricing policies. Also, since price directly affects trade revenues and salespeople's commissions, it can be used to foster the desired behaviors.

Developing a Price Structure

Price administration deals with price adjustments or price differentials for sales made under different conditions, such as:

• sales made in different quantities

• sales made to different types of middlemen performing different functions

• sales made to buyers in different geographic locations

• sales made with different credit and collection policies

• sales made at different times of the day, month, season, or year.

Essentially, price structure decisions define how differential characteristics of the product and/or service will be priced. They are of strategic importance to manufacturers, distributors or dealers, and retailers. In establishing a price structure there are many possible ways of antagonizing distributors and even incurring legal liability. It is necessary to avoid these dangers while at the same time using the price structure to achieve the desired profit objectives.

Consider the problem of developing a price for taxi service. There are a number of ways of pricing taxi services, including:

• a fixed charge to enter the taxi plus a variable fee per mile and/or minute (e.g. $0.50 plus $1 per mile traveled, or $1 per minute in transit)

• a fixed charge within the zone area of pickup, plus a fee for each zone boundary crossed

• variable fee per mile

• fixed charge per passenger plus any one of the above fee schedules

• differential fees for rush hour vs non-rush hour service.

Or consider the airlines who may set a ticket price based on one or more of type of itinerary, time of day, day of week, length of stay at destination, when reservation is made or class of service. Thus there are many alternative ways to price a product or service depending on its characteristics, who is making the purchase, when the purchase occurs, when payment is made, the volume being purchased, or where the buyer is located. Regardless of its degree of complexity or simplicity, a pricing decision also requires the development of a price structure.

Offering different products or services in the line with different features or benefits at different prices permits the opportunity to develop prices for buyers who have different degrees of sensitivity to price levels and price differences. Moving from a simple "one price for all buyers" structure to a more complex pricing structure provides for pricing flexibility, because the complexity permits price variations based on specific product and service characteristics as well as buyer or market differences. Moreover, a more complex price structure enhances the ability of firms to:

• respond to specific competitive threats or opportunities

• enhance revenues while minimizing revenue loss due to price changes

• manage the costs of delivering the product or service

• develop focused price changes

• be more effective in gaining distributors' cooperation.

To link pricing strategy to overall marketing strategy requires recognition of price structure as a valuable aspect of pricing and marketing strategy. Then decision makers need to determine how prices should vary across customers, products, territories, and purchase occasions to meet corporate objectives. To accomplish this goal of differential pricing requires the key factors differentiating price-market segments to be identified. Then the elements of the price structure may be developed to reflect these factors.

An Overview of Discount Decisions

A *product's list price* is the product's price to final buyers. Throughout the distribution system, manufacturers grant intermediaries *discounts*, or deductions from the list price. These price concessions from producers may be seen as payment to intermediaries for performing the distribution function and for providing time and place utilities. The difference between the list price and the amount the original producer receives represents the total discounts provided to channel members. Channel members themselves employ discounts in various ways. Wholesalers pass on discounts to retailers just as manufacturers pass along discounts to wholesalers. Retailers may offer promotional discounts to consumers in the form of sweepstakes, contests, and free samples. Some stores offer quantity and cash discounts to regular customers. Even seasonal discounts may be passed along—for example, to reduce inventory of Halloween candy or Christmas cards. Exhibit 6 describes the six primary forms of discounts: trade, functional, quantity, cash, promotional, and seasonal. Exhibit 7 calculates the discounts for a product qualifying for all types of price reduction; the discounts are figured backward from the manufacturer's suggested list price.

EXHIBIT 6
CHARACTERISTICS OF MAJOR DISCOUNTS

Trade and Functional Discounts

Trade discounts are based on a distributor's place in the distributive sequence while functional discounts represent payment for performing certain marketing functions. Although we are accustomed to think of price as a single number, it is usually quoted to distributors as a series of numbers, for example: '30, 10, 5 and 2/10, net 30' or '30, 20, 5, and 2/10, net EOM (end of month).' The first three numbers represent successive discounts from the list or base price. The list price usually designates the approximate or suggested final selling price of a product and is the price usually referred to when discussing the methods of price determination.

The justification for functional discounts is that different distributors perform different functions within the distribution channel and should be compensated accordingly. For example, some wholesalers provide storage facilities for the manufacturer, help the retailer set up displays, extend credit to the retailer, as well as perform personal selling services for the manufacturer.

Quantity Discounts

Perhaps the most common type of discount is the *quantity discount*. Such a discount is granted for volume purchases (measured in dollars or units), either in a single purchase (*non-cumulative*) or over a specified period of time (*cumulative, deferred* or *patronage discount*). The discount schedule may specify a single product or a limited number of products, or the discount may allow for a complete mix of products ordered in a single purchase or over a period of time.

Non-cumulative quantity discounts serve to encourage large orders, leading to fewer orders over a given period. This ordering policy benefits sellers because they have fewer orders to process, ship, and invoice, thereby reducing total costs for these activities. Cumulative discounts do not have these benefits, but they do tend to tie a buyer to a seller over the discount period, if the buyer is anxious to obtain the discount. Sometimes the nature of the product makes it advantageous to place small orders, for example perishable products and large consumer durables or heavy equipment and machinery. For these kinds of products, buying in small quantities is practical and a cumulative discount schedule is beneficial to both parties.

Cash Discounts

A *cash discount* is a reward for the payment of an invoice or account within a specified period of time. Even though cash discounts are usually small, they add up for buyers who make many or large purchases. Producers offer such price reductions to encourage prompt payments and improve their cashflow.

Promotional Discounts

A *promotional discount* is given to distributors as an allowance for the distributors' efforts to promote the manufacturer's product through local advertising, special displays, or other promotions. These allowances may take the form of a percentage reduction in the price paid, additional merchandise (e.g. a free case for every dozen cases ordered), or they may be an outright cash payment either to the distributor or to the promotional vehicle, e.g. a local newspaper.

Seasonal Discounts

Air conditioners, resort hotel space, greeting cards and home insulation all have strong seasonal demand. To keep production facilities operating year-round and to shift storage charges into the distribution channel, producers of such goods may offer seasonal discounts to off-season buyers.

EXHIBIT 7
CALCULATION OF POSSIBLE DISCOUNTS

List price (producer's suggested selling price):		$100.00
Discounts:		
Functional	33%	
Quantity	10%	
Cash	3%	
Seasonal	3%	
Promotional	6%	
Price paid to producer:		
list price		$100.00
less functional discount ($100.00 x 33%)	-33.00	
	$67.00	
less quantity discount ($67.00 x 10%)	-6.70	
	$60.30	
less promotional discount ($60.30 x 6%)	-3.62	
	$56.68	
less seasonal discount ($56.68 x 3%)	-1.70	
	$54.98	
less cash discount ($54.98 x 3%)	-1.65	
	$53.33	
Final price paid to producer by intermediary:		$53.33
Total dollar discount:		$46.67
Total discount percentage:		46.67%

Summary

1. Managing the pricing function involves setting prices and determining when price adjustments should be made for selling in different quantities, to different types of middlemen, in different geographic locations, and for sales made with different terms of payment.

2. Manufacturers allow intermediaries deductions from the list price in the form of discounts. There are five primary types of discounts: functional, quantity, cash, promotional, seasonal.

By the end of Step 7 the audit team will have:

• developed a pricing structure

• made decisions in relation to discounts.

Part 2

THE AUDIT
PROCESS

This section addresses the logistical and process requirements of conducting an audit. The topics covered in this section include:

- Staffing the audit team

- Creating an audit project plan

- Laying the groundwork for the audit

- Analyzing audit results

- Sharing audit results

- Writing effective audit reports

- Dealing with resistance to audit recommendations

- Building an ongoing audit program

STAFFING THE AUDIT TEAM

Who conducts the audit is as important in many ways as how the audit is conducted. In fact, the people selected for the audit team will, in large part, determine how the audit is done, how results are analyzed, and how findings are reported. The following list includes general characteristics of effective audit teams for most areas:

- Consists of three to four people.

- Reports to CEO or other senior executive.

- Represents a carefully selected range of skills and experience.

More than four people may be needed for an audit team if data gathering is labor intensive, as when large numbers of customers or employees must be interviewed. However, audit teams of more than six or seven people present problems of maintaining uniformity and communicating audit progress and findings during the course of the evaluation.

Selecting an Audit Team Leader

The audit team leader will play a strong role in shaping both the data gathering and the findings from the audit. The strength of the team leader will also influence the acceptance of the audit, both in terms of enlisting cooperation in the data gathering phase and in securing support for improvement initiatives that grow out of the audit. Because of the importance of this role, care should be taken in selecting the appropriate person for the job. The following qualities are found in successful audit team leaders:

- Has a good relationship with the CEO or with the executive-level sponsor of the audit.

- Is well-liked and well-respected at all levels of the organization, especially in the area to be audited.

- Has good interpersonal skills; can maintain good relationships even in difficult circumstances.

- Has good analytical skills; can assimilate and process large amounts of complex data quickly.

- Has some knowledge of the function or area being audited.

- Has extensive knowledge of the type of process being audited.

- Communicates ideas clearly and effectively.

Skills to Be Represented on the Audit Team

Once the team leader has been chosen, audit team members should be selected on the basis of what each can bring to the project. Selection efforts should focus on developing a balanced representation of the following qualities:

- A variety of tenures in the organization, with relative newcomers preferably having experience in other organizations.

- A variety of familiarity with the area (function or site) being audited. Those who are intimately familiar with the area can serve as guides to the less familiar; those who are new to the area can provide objectivity and ask questions that might never be considered by those more involved in the area.

- Considerable familiarity with the type of process being audited. For this reason, many organizations call on people filling roles in similar processes from other parts of the company to work on audit teams.

- Good analytical skills.

- Good interpersonal skills.

- Good facilitation and interviewing skills.

- Good communication skills.

- An understanding of the company's strategy and direction.

CREATING AN AUDIT PROJECT PLAN

Creating an audit project plan accomplishes the following objectives:

- Ensures the allocation of adequate resources, or helps audit team members be prepared to improvise in the face of short resources.

- Ensures the audit is timed so resources are available that may be in high demand.

- Creates clear expectations in the minds of team members about what must be done, and when — especially important when they are not committed to the project full-time.

- Ensures accountability for what must be done, who is responsible for which tasks, and when the audit must be completed.

Financial audits often rely on the Critical Path Method (CPM) of project planning. This method was originally developed by the US Department of Defense during World War II to facilitate the timely completion of weapons development and production. It has since been modified to plan a wide variety of projects. The following outline is a simplification of CPM. It suggests the aspects of a project that should be taken into account during the planning phase.

Critical Path Method

In developing the project plan, audit team members should ask and answer the following questions:

- *What tasks must be performed?*

This list should include the major tasks outlined in the audits, along with subtasks that grow out of those major headings. It should also include any tasks mandated by unique circumstances in the company performing the self-assessment. The audit team may want to brainstorm about tasks that need to be performed, then refine the list to reflect the work priorities of the audit.

- *In what order will the tasks be completed?*

Answering this question should include an analysis of which tasks and sub tasks are dependent on others. Which tasks cannot begin until another has been completed? Which tasks can be done at any time? The audit team may want to place the ordered task on a time line, with start dates, expected duration of the step, and end dates outlined for each task.

- *Who will perform each task?*

Most tasks will be performed by members of the audit team. These assignments should be made by taking the strengths of each team member into consideration, as well as the time availability of each person. Equity of work load should also be taken into account. If tasks are to be assigned to people not on the audit team, those individuals should be included or consulted at this point.

- *What resources will be needed for each step?*

Each task should be analyzed in terms of the personnel, budget, equipment, facilities, support services, and any other resources that will be needed for its completion. The team should assess the availability of all of the resources. Consideration should be given to the task ordering completed earlier. Are some resources subject to competing demands, and therefore difficult to secure at a particular time? How far in advance do arrangements for resources need to be made? Does the task order or time line need to be revised in light of what is known about resource availability?

- *Where is the slack time?*

Slack time is unscheduled time between dependent tasks. Slack provides a degree of flexibility in altering the start dates of subsequent tasks. Slack time signals that a task has a range of possible start dates. It is used to determine the critical path.

- *What is the critical path?*

The critical path in a project is the set of tasks that must be completed in a sequential, chronological order. If any task on the critical path is not completed, all subsequent tasks will be delayed. Delays at any point in the critical path will result in an equivalent delay in the completion of the total project.

Regardless of the method used to develop the project plan, no project, regardless how simple, is ever completed in exact accordance with its plan. However, having a project plan allows the team to gauge its progress, anticipate problems and determine where alternative approaches are needed.

LAYING THE GROUNDWORK FOR THE AUDIT

Once the team has been selected and a project plan developed, the audit leader should prepare those who will be involved in and affected by the audit for the team's visit or for data-gathering. The following steps will help the audit to run more smoothly:

Communicate Executive Support for the Audit

Demonstrating executive support for the audit accomplishes two goals. First, it increases the chances that those involved in the area being audited will cooperate with data gathering efforts. Second, it shows executive support for the area being audited and suggests a commitment to improving the area's performance.

In many companies, the audit is introduced by the executive sponsor of the audit by means of a memo. The memo should explain the purpose of the audit and ask for the support of everyone in the area being audited. This memo is distributed to everyone within the company who will be affected by or involved in the data gathering process. The most effective memos explain how the audit results will be used, reassuring those who will be responding to audit team requests about the motives of the audit. The credibility of such memos is also bolstered when previous audits have been acted upon with positive results.

Make Arrangements with the Area to Be Audited

The audit team leader should check with the appropriate manager in charge of the process or site being audited to arrange for any required on-site visits, interviewing, surveys, focus groups, or written information needed for the audit. The team leader should also explain the purpose, scope, and expected duration of the audit; review the project plan with the manager; and answer any questions the manager has about the audit.

The team leader should also work with the appropriate manager or managers to determine how the audit can be conducted with the least impact on the flow of work. This may include discussions about the timing of the audit, the options for data gathering, the availability of needed data, and possibilities for generating the necessary information quickly and easily. Finding ways to make data collection more efficient and effective is especially important when the audit is part of an ongoing program, rather than an isolated assessment.

Develop a Protocol or Checklist

A protocol or checklist can be used by the audit team to outline the issues that are central to the audit. Written guides can help the leaders of those areas being audited to prepare for the audit. A protocol represents a plan of what the audit team will do to accomplish the objectives of the audit. It is an important tool of the audit, since it not only serves as the audit team's guide to collecting data, but also as a record of the audit procedures completed by the team. In some cases, audit teams may even want to format the checklist in a way that allows them to record their field notes directly on the checklist.

The checklist should include no more than twenty major items, and checklists should be updated with each audit in order to ensure that the appropriate measures are taken. Items where improvement initiatives have been successful should be eliminated from the checklist, with newly identified possibilities for improvement opportunities added.

ANALYZING
AUDIT RESULTS

Discovering gaps between a company's targets and its actual performance is a relatively easy task. Tools are provided to assist audit teams in assessing their performance in a given area. In most cases, more opportunities for improvement will be uncovered by an audit than can be addressed by the resources and energy available. Therefore, one of the most difficult aspects of analyzing the results of an audit lies in determining which opportunities are the most important for managers to pursue.

Because resources and energy for pursuing improvement initiatives are limited, choices must be made about which options are most important. Sometimes these decisions are based on political winds in the company, or on what has worked well in the past, or on personal preferences of top management. However, scarce resources will be used more effectively if allocated to the areas where they will have the greatest impact. Managers must also determine the most effective way to approach initiatives. This section discusses criteria for prioritizing opportunities that grow out of audit findings.

The Novations Strategic Alignment Model

The mid-1980s saw the birth of the "excellence" movement, where many companies tried to achieve excellence in every area of endeavour. Although the movement created an awareness of the need for management improvements, it failed to consider that not all management processes are equal in terms of producing benefits. As a result, leading organizations in today's environment focus on performing well in a few core areas. Knowing what those core areas are depends on a clear vision of the company's strategy.

Strategic thinking about which areas should be improved involves much more than taking an inventory of current capabilities and weaknesses. If it did not, existing capabilities would always determine strategic objectives, and organizational growth and development would come to a halt. To set priorities strategically, companies must decide which improvement opportunities fall in the following categories:

- What to do themselves.

- What to do with someone else.

- What to contract others to do.

- What not to do.

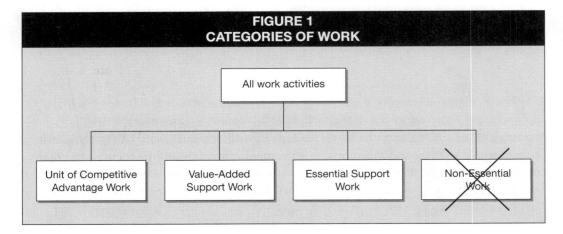

Figure 1 illustrates the four categories of work.

Unit of Competitive Advantage (UCA) Work includes work and capabilities that create distinctiveness for the business in the marketplace.

Value-added Support Work facilitates the accomplishment of the UCA work. For example, a company may have a technology orientation rather than a service orientation, but an effective logistics process may help them to improve their UCA work of providing cutting edge technology.

Essential Support Work neither creates advantage nor facilitates the work that creates advantage, but must be done if businesses are to continue to operate (includes such things as paying taxes, maintaining payroll records, etc.).

Nonessential Work is activity that has lost its usefulness but continues to be done because of tradition.

Despite their sophistication in dealing with other aspects of business, most managers have archaic views of the different types of work. Many of their models for characterizing work have come from a finance or accounting orientation. Accounting terms such as overhead, direct labor, and indirect labor may be useful as a way to report costs, but they provide little understanding about the relative strategic importance of the work. Yet these classifications are frequently used to determine how work is organized and where resources are allocated.

The concept of unit of competitive advantage (UCA) helps to explain why some organizations either emphasize the wrong capabilities or de-emphasize the right capabilities. UCA also explains why some forms of improvement lead to competitive disadvantage, and why some businesses consistently outperform their competitors by gaining greater leverage from their competitive advantages.

A company's UCA includes the critical processes that create distinctiveness within an established strategic direction. It is based on the premise that businesses create competitive advantage when they focus their attention on a few key processes and implement those key processes in world-class fashion. For example, continuous improvement is a popular management program that assumes benefit from any kind of ongoing improvement. Generally speaking, however, continuous improvement program will only create competitive advantage when an organization defines a strategic direction, clarifies strategic objectives, and determines its UCA. These crucial prerequisites tell where continuous improvement efforts should be focused to create maximum leverage. They suggest what kinds of work to improve interdependently, what kinds to improve separately, and what kinds not to waste time on. They even signal when continuous improvement is more likely to create competitive disadvantage rather than competitive advantage.

UCA Initiatives Should Take Priority

Understanding what work falls under which categories requires a clear understanding of the company's strategy. The initiatives resulting from an audit that affect the Unit of Competitive Advantage work processes should clearly have the highest priority among improvement projects. Value-added support initiatives should be second priority, and essential support work should be the third priority. Nonessential work should not be continued.

Once improvement opportunities that will have the greatest impact on the achievement of the company's goals have been identified, the following ideas can be used to lend further insight into how opportunities identified through an audit should be prioritized:

- *Focus on the two or three most important areas.*

Insisting that action be taken on all of the problems uncovered by the audit may overwhelm the people who are responsible for bringing about those changes. Flatter organizations and leaner work forces mean that people are already being asked to do more work with fewer resources and less time. Producing a long list of improvement initiatives may prompt people to dismiss all of them because they don't have time to complete the whole list.

- *Focus on the areas that can be changed.*

Emphasizing problems that are beyond the control of the people who are responsible to work on process improvement only leads to cynicism and a sense of powerlessness. By focusing on things that are within the sphere of influence, accountability for each part of the action plan can be clearly defined.

• *Include as priorities some improvements that can be made quickly.*

Rapid, visible improvement helps build support for more complicated initiatives. Quick improvements also reassure people of management's support for long-term improvement. Seeing immediate improvement helps to build commitment at all levels to the process, and helps build momentum for further change.

• *Emphasize the improvements that seem essential to long-term success.*

Essential improvements may involve sensitive issues or difficult problems, such as deficiencies in fundamental skill levels within the organization or basic strategy issues. These problems are not only difficult and expensive to address, but may also cause a great deal of personal pain or require significant individual adjustment. Nevertheless, long-term improvement requires a commitment to dealing with difficult issues rather than avoiding them.

SHARING AUDIT RESULTS

In most cases, audit results will be presented to various interested people in a feedback meeting. Those in attendance may include members of the executive team, managers who work in the area covered by the audit, the audit team members, and anyone else who is affected by or interested in the results. The meeting should be conducted by members of the audit team. The purpose is to present their findings, and make recommendations for capitalizing on opportunities for improvement.

Conducting Effective Feedback Meetings

The audit team's strategy for the meeting should be to present a clear and simple picture of the current situation as revealed by the audit. This may be a moment of truth for those who have been anticipating the audit results. The feedback meeting for an audit holds both excitement and anxiety: excitement that the future will be bright, and anxiety that shortcomings in individual performance will be highlighted and demands made for personal change. As a result, the meeting must be carefully managed in order to lead to productive change. The following structure is one recommended format for conducting a feedback meeting.

- *Introduce the meeting and preview its agenda.*

This might include an overview of the original intent of the audit, introduction of the audit team, and a brief summary of the meeting's agenda. This step should take no more than five minutes.

- *Present the audit findings.*

Audit findings should summarize the most important points revealed by the data gathered in the audit process. They should be presented separately from the audit recommendations in order to allow people to digest the two parts of the presentation separately. Clearing up misunderstandings about the findings may make the group more accepting of the team's recommendations.

The presentation of the audit findings should take comparatively little time. Audits almost always generate much more data than can be effectively presented or digested in a feedback meeting. The goal of the audit team should be to zero in on the two or three most important points learned from the audit, and present enough supporting data to illustrate those points.

Presenting too much data about audit findings has a number of negative effects. It encourages people to conduct their own analysis of the audit data. To a certain extent, this is a healthy and normal reaction. If others understand the evidence that supports the conclusions drawn by the audit team, they are more likely to accept and own the audit results. Therefore, they will be more committed to the changes brought about by the audit results. However, when people immerse themselves in large amounts of data, they may become victims of "analysis paralysis": they may spend unnecessary time attempting to explain contradictory data, or trying to understand methods used by others to gather data.

- *Present audit recommendations.*

Presenting the audit recommendations should be the central point of the meeting. The recommendations should grow out of the data highlights presented. The audit team should view the recommendations as discussion points for the meeting, rather than as absolute action items.

A common mistake in feedback meetings is to spend most of the meeting on presenting data and recommendations. It is easy for audit team members to become enamored of data they have invested considerable time and energy to collect and analyze. Others in the audience will probably also be interested in the details of the data collected. However, if too much time is spent on discussing the recommendations, the meeting will end before a commitment to action has been made.

- *Ask others to react to the data.*

The reactions of top management and those responsible for implementing audit recommendations will determine the ultimate value of the audit data. Therefore, the feedback meeting is a good time to resolve questions or problems with the findings and recommendations as they have been presented. If resistance to the audit findings is not resolved in the feedback meeting, opportunities for improvement may be lost.

Those attending the meeting may offer their opinions willingly. If not, the audit team members should ask the others in the room for their reaction to what has been presented.

- *Develop preliminary action plans.*

The detailed action plans should grow out of the recommendations made by the audit team. They should specifically address the question of who should do what by when. Formal accountability mechanisms should be established before the end of the meeting, such as the scheduling of subsequent meetings or follow-up check points.

WRITING EFFECTIVE AUDIT REPORTS

There are three fundamental purposes for writing a formal report at the conclusion of an audit:

- An audit report may be a stand-alone summary of the audit. This approach is not recommended, inasmuch as the report is likely to be filed away, making the probability of action unlikely.

- The report may supplement a feedback meeting, providing those in attendance with documentation and an outline to follow.

- The report should also serve as a baseline document to make measurement of performance improvement possible in future audits.

Because the written report is the most enduring part of the audit presentation, it should be well written and easy to understand. The following tips will lead to the preparation of effective written audit reports.

Focus on a Few Key Points

The audit presentation should focus on the two or three most important findings. It is impossible to present all of the data gathered in the audit to those who were not on the audit team. It is also not advisable to present every detail of the data. The audit team members should trust their own judgment about what the highlights of the study were, and present enough data to support that judgment. For each of the major findings, the team may want to include the following information:

- What is the problem?

- Why does it exist?

- What happens if the problem is not fixed:

  — in the short term?

  — in the long term?

- Recommend solutions.

- Outline expected benefits.

Prepare an Outline Before Writing the First Draft

A good outline ensures that the logic of the report is clear, and that ideas proceed in an order that makes sense. The following outline provides one approach that works effectively.

Background

This section should establish the framework for the audit in terms of:

- Providing a brief discussion of the overall purpose of the audit.

- Identifying the role of the audit team in the overall process.

- Establishing the limitations of the audit methodology to ensure that others utilize the results provided in the report appropriately.

Objectives

This section should identify specific objectives of the audit in terms of types of information the team was expected to generate.

Methodology

The methodology section should describe the mechanics of the audit and include the following information:

- Types of assessment used (survey, interviews, focus groups, etc.).

- Data sources, or the sample groups for each of the types of assessment used.

- Time frame during which the audit was conducted.

- Other pertinent details about how the audit was conducted.

Findings

This section is designed to provide others with a review of the "facts" that came out of the audit. Except in cases where an audit checks regulatory compliance, only the most significant findings should be discussed in any detail in the report. This section should also include briefly presented data supporting the findings.

Conclusions

This section should report the audit team's interpretation of what the facts of the audit mean in light of the objectives stated at the outset of the audit.

Recommendations

This section includes suggestions from the audit team on how to close the performance gaps identified in the audit. The degree of specificity to be included in the audit report will vary from company to company and audit to audit.

Appendix

This portion of the formal report should include any of the following items that are relevant to the audit:

- A copy of any questionnaires or survey instruments used in the audit.

- A summary of the data gathered in the course of the audit.

- Recommendations for subsequent audits based on the team's experience.

Present Audit Findings Accurately

Those who read the report will no doubt be somewhat familiar with the area covered by the audit. They may notice discrepancies between what they know about the subject and what is reported in the written document. Spotting one inaccuracy may lead the readers to discredit all of the findings, conclusions and recommendations. Audit team members should be careful to report data as it was actually generated, and to describe the impact of the findings accurately.

Use Clear, Concise Language

Every statement included in the report should be based on sound evidence developed or reviewed during the audit. Whatever is said must be supported or supportable. Speculation should be avoided. Generalities and vague reporting will only confuse and mislead those that the report should influence or inform. For example, a report using the terms some, a few, or not all can leave the reader confused about the significance of the finding. Specific quantities should be used, such as, "of the ten samples taken, two were found to be…", "Three of five respondents said that…", and so on. Statements should be qualified as needed, and any unconfirmed data or information should be identified as such.

Ideas or sentences that do not amplify the central theme should be eliminated. The report should not identify individuals or highlight the mistakes of individuals.

Use Good Grammar and Style

Basic grammar and style rules should be followed in writing the text. Below are some examples:

- Avoid extreme terms, such as alarming, deplorable, gross negligence, etc.

- Avoid using redundant or lengthy phrases, such as calling something an emergency situation when the word emergency alone will do.

- Avoid verbs camouflaged as nouns or adjectives. For example, use "the new procedure will reduce error entries," rather than "The new procedure will accomplish a reduction of error entries."

- Avoid indirect expressions where possible. For example, "Many instances of poor management were found," is more direct than saying, "There were many instances of poor judgment found."

- Use short, familiar words. Use words that are easily understandable to everyone and that convey the message concisely.

- Keep sentences short. Most writing experts suggest that an average sentence should be between 15 and 18 words. Packing too many ideas into a single sentence confuses and tires readers.

The audit team should provide enough background information in the report so that the reader clearly understands who conducted the audit and what the audit did or did not include. The purpose of the report as well as the purpose and scope of the audit should also be described in a manner that enables the reader to know why the report was written and who should take corrective action.

Timing of the Report

The timing of audit reports is critical to the overall reporting process and must be carefully thought out. In many cases, a written draft of the audit report is prepared one to three weeks before the feedback meeting. This draft then goes through a review and another report is prepared in time for the team's presentation. A final report may be completed after the feedback session has been held in order to record changes resulting from that meeting.

DEALING WITH RESISTANCE TO RECOMMENDATIONS

Most audit teams feel that if they can present their ideas clearly and logically, and have the best interests of the company or department at heart, managers will accept the recommendations made as part of the audit and follow the team's recommendations. Many people who have worked in organizations, however, find that no matter how reasonably recommendations are presented, they are all too often not implemented.

Implementation usually fails because it requires people to change their ways of working. That change requires a great deal of effort, energy, and risk; therefore, change is usually resisted. Resistance is an emotional process; people may embrace recommendations based on their logic, but fail to implement them because of the emotional resistance to the personal change involved. Resistance is a predictable, natural, and necessary part of the learning process. Although resistance may cause audit team members to feel they have missed the mark in terms of the recommendations they have made, it actually often signals accuracy in having interpreted the organization's needs. By dealing with the resistance directly, audit teams can work through barriers to implementing process improvements.

What Are the Signs of Resistance?

In many cases, resistance may be expressed directly. Direct objections to recommendations are relatively easy to address, inasmuch as they can be discussed and resolved. When recommendations are being presented, team members should stop frequently to allow those who are listening to the report to voice any objections or disagreements. Those who are presenting the data should be careful not to become defensive or to punish those who express reservations about the recommendations. It is impossible to deal with objections unless they are voiced; therefore, the audit team should welcome the expression of objections or differences of opinion. The following tips may be used for surfacing and dealing with direct resistance:

- Provide many opportunities for others to express their concerns.

- Carefully clarify any confusing concerns.

- Deal with important or easy concerns immediately. Defer the remainder.

- Summarize the concerns before moving on. Show that concerns have been heard.

- It may even be helpful to list concerns on a flip chart or blackboard.

If direct resistance continues, the following steps may be necessary:

- Talk about the differences of opinion.

- Voice concern and support for negotiating a resolution.

- Avoid struggles for control of the situation.

Dealing with Indirect Resistance

In other cases, resistance may be subtle and elusive. Indirect resistance is difficult to identify and deal with because its manifestations seem logical. People who are experiencing indirect resistance may feel that they are "getting the run around." Many different forms of resistance may manifest themselves in a single meeting:

- Request for more detail.

- Providing too much detail in response to questions.

- Complaining that there isn't enough time to implement recommendations.

- Claiming that the recommendations are impractical.

- Attacking those who propose improvement initiatives.

- Acting confused.

- Responding with silence.

- Intellectualizing about the data.

- Moralizing that problems wouldn't exist if it weren't for "those people".

- Agreeing to implement recommendations with no intention of acting on them.

- Asking questions about methodology.

- Arguing that previous problems have resolved themselves.

- Focusing on solutions before findings are fully understood.

Almost any of these responses is legitimate in moderate amounts. For example, members of the group may have concerns about the audit's methodology that should be considered. Managers may realistically wonder where they will find the time to implement recommendations. However, if refusal to act on recommendations persists once legitimate concerns have been addressed, then the audit team is probably facing indirect resistance.

Many models used in sales training provide recommendations for overcoming resistance. These methods suggest the use of data and logical arguments to win the point and convince the other person to buy whatever is being sold. These models work well for direct resistance. However, indirect resistance is normally based on feelings rather than logic. Therefore, the only way to truly overcome resistance is to deal with the emotional processes that cause it to happen in the first place. It is almost impossible to talk people out of the way they feel.

Feelings pass and change when they are expressed directly. A key skill for audit teams that are attempting to implement recommendations is to ask the people who are presenting resistance to put directly into words what they are experiencing. The most effective way to make this happen is for the audit team members to address directly what is happening in the situation. The following keys provide help in surfacing and dealing with indirect resistance.

- *Work once or twice with the person's concern, even when it feels as if he or she is resisting recommendations.*

By attempting to work with the problem stated by the person raising a concern, audit team members can determine whether the concern is legitimate or whether it is an excuse for not taking action. If the issues raised are legitimate, the person should show some willingness to discuss and resolve them. If the issues are manifestations of indirect resistance, the person will probably respond with other forms of resistance.

- *Identify the form the resistance is taking.*

Paying attention to the dynamics of a discussion can provide important clues as to whether or not a person is resisting recommendations. If a person is consistently distancing him or herself from those who are presenting the audit findings, using gestures or postures that suggest tension or discomfort, while at the same time presenting arguments for why the recommendations presented are inappropriate, it is probably a sign of resistance. The non-verbal responses of the presenters may also signal the onset of resistance. If presenters feel that they are suppressing negative feelings or becoming bored or irritated, it may be further evidence that the client is resisting.

Once presenters become aware of the resistance, the next step is to put it into words. This is best done by using neutral, everyday language. The skill is to describe the form of the resistance in a way that encourages the person to make a more direct statement of the reservation he or she is experiencing.

One general rule for stating what type of resistance is being manifested is to phrase the statement in common, non-threatening language. Statements should be made in the same tone and language that would be used to address a problem with a spouse or close friend. The statement should be made with as little evaluation as possible; it is the presenter's observation about what is happening in the situation.

A second general rule for surfacing indirect resistance involves not talking for a couple of moments after the presenter has stated what he or she has observed. There may be a temptation to elaborate on the observation, or to support it with evidence. However, continuing the statement will reduce the tension in the situation. Without tension, the person who is resisting feels no discomfort, and is unlikely to address the issue directly. Moreover, elaborating on the original statement may increase the other person's defensiveness and reduce the chances of solving the problem.

If stating the problem in direct, non-punishing terms fails to bring the resistance out into the open, there may be little more the audit team can do to overcome the indirect resistance. The best strategy in this case is to avoid resisting the resistance. Team members should support the person who is resisting and proceed with the implementation of recommendations to the extent possible.

BUILDING AN ONGOING AUDIT PROGRAM

As the pace of change increases, and as organization leaders become more and more committed to continuously improving their effectiveness and efficiency, audits of all types of processes will become more common. The most effective companies will establish program of ongoing audits, whereby a number of goals can be accomplished:

- Performance improvements can be measured over time.

- Important changes in the company's environment can be systematically monitored.

- Managers can make a habit of change and improvement, rather than resisting it.

- Those areas that are of highest importance to the company can be routinely improved.

- Processes can be modified to be in alignment with changes in strategy or in the environment.

As with all management techniques, however, an enduring program of ongoing audits requires that audits become integrated into the overall management system. The following guidelines are keys to weaving audits into the fabric of day-to-day operations.

Establish Support for Ongoing Audits

While support for audits begins at the executive level, ownership for the audit process must be felt throughout the organization if an ongoing program is to be successful. The following actions will help to broaden support for the audit process, while ensuring greater benefit from the audit.

- *Share the results of the audit with everyone throughout the organization.*

By keeping others informed about the results of an audit, managers reassure those who participate in and are affected by the audit of the integrity of the process. Employees sometimes become suspicious of probing investigators; they may have doubts about how the information will be used, or whether the information will be used. By sharing audit results, managers make an implicit commitment to improving the processes that have been evaluated.

- *Act on the audit results.*

Questions will be raised about continuing audits if early assessments bear no fruits. Failing to act on performance gaps that are identified leads to cynicism and lack of trust among those who work with the problems daily. On the other hand, improving a process can create the momentum that comes from accomplishment. Committing resources and attention to the improvement opportunities revealed by an audit also shows management commitment to the improvement process.

- *Let others know when performance has improved.*

Communicating the positive results from an audit is one way of rewarding the people who contributed to that improvement. It also builds faith in the effectiveness of the audit process. Moreover, showing that performance has improved is another means of reassuring people of a commitment to the improvement process.

- *Reward people for their part in improvements.*

Increasing efficiency and effectiveness can often be a threatening experience for those who are involved in a work process. Improving the way resources are used often means eliminating the need for some of the people who have been involved in the process. Although flatter, leaner organizations often preclude the possibility of offering promotions, managers should nevertheless attempt to ensure that people who contribute to performance improvement find their own situations better rather than worse as a result.

Rewards for helping to close performance gaps may span a range from thanking people for their efforts to planning a group celebration to offering bonuses or pay increases for improvement. Rewards are especially meaningful when people are allowed to suggest what rewards they would like for their contribution. This may provide managers with new ideas for rewards that may be less costly to the organization than financial recognition.

- *Involve a wide variety of people in the audit process.*

People can be involved in the audit process in many ways. By involving people from a broad spectrum, more people learn about audit techniques and results, thus spreading commitment to the audit process throughout the organization. By involving many people in the data-gathering process, employees feel that action plans growing out of the audit were a result of their input. Excluding people from the data-gathering phase usually reduces the feeling of ownership for the results, thus making people feel as if initiatives are being imposed on them. By the same token, involving a broad range of people in the development of action plans expands ownership for the plans and allows for the generation of more ideas.

Part 3

IMPLEMENTING A PRICING STRATEGY AUDIT: QUESTIONS AND CHECKLISTS

This section of the Pricing Strategy Audit comprises a series of questions based on the seven steps given in Part 1. These questions have been designed to help you plan and implement your audit in a straightforward and practical manner, covering all the relevant parts of the audit in the correct sequence.

THE SEVEN STEPS OF A PRICING STRATEGY AUDIT

- Step 1 Assess the Consistency Between Corporate and Pricing Objectives

- Step 2 Assess the Relevant Economics for the Pricing Strategy

- Step 3 Determine How Your Buyers Perceive Prices

- Step 4 Determine the Relevant Costs for the Pricing Strategy

- Step 5 Determine the Characteristics of Each Specific Price Decision

- Step 6 Integrate Specific Price Decisions into an Overall Pricing Strategy

- Step 7 Assess the Administrative Structure for Managing the Pricing Function

Note: Before you look at these questions, you may like to look at the *Introduction to Pricing* and the *Guidelines for Developing Effective Pricing Strategies and Tactics* and the front of the Pricing Strategy Audit. The introduction outlines the role and definition of pricing, looks at proactive pricing and also covers the factors to consider when setting prices. The guidelines run through the setting up of an audit team, the four basic rules of pricing, adaptive pricing and provides the key considerations for better pricing decisions.

ASSESS THE CONSISTENCY BETWEEN CORPORATE AND PRICING OBJECTIVES

BACKGROUND INFORMATION

Pricing strategy objectives should be derived from two prior levels of planning.

Level 1. Overall corporate objectives.
Level 2. Specific marketing objectives.

Pricing objectives need to be classified according to three factors.

1. Profitability or financial goals.

2. Sales volume.

3. Competition.

Once these objectives have been set, they should be measured against current performance and overall corporate goals.

In the "Questions" section below you will find a set of questions for classifying your pricing objectives.

QUESTIONS

1. Profitability or financial goals

- Have profitability objectives been expressed in dollars or as a percentage of sales?

- In order to maximize profit, does the company aim for low prices, high turnover and high sales volume, or higher prices, a reduced turnover and higher profits?

- Has the company adopted the common pricing objective of target return on investment?

2. Sales volume

- Have pricing objectives been set in terms of sales volume?

- If so, has the goal been sales growth or sales maintenance?

- When considering the product mix alongside the company's strategic orientations, have prices been set high or low?

- Do the company's pricing objectives match its marketing objectives?

3. Competition

- Given the company's competitive strategies, is the goal to achieve price stability and engage in non-price competition or to price aggressively?

Having set the pricing objectives and measured performance and corporate goals against them, it is now necessary to use economic principles to analyze pricing decisions and understand how pricing works. These principles are outlined in Step 2. A brief list of appropriate audit questions follows an outline of this step.

ASSESS THE RELEVANT ECONOMICS FOR THE PRICING STRATEGY

BACKGROUND INFORMATION

Product demand is one of the most vital cornerstones of price determination, especially in terms of the volume of a product the buyer is prepared to purchase at a given price.

In order to make pricing decisions, the discipline of economics provides four essential analytical concepts.

1. Demand elasticity.

2. Revenue concepts.

3. Consumers' surplus.

4. Signals.

Note: It is also important to remember that product buyers often use price both as an indicator of product cost and of product quality, even when other product information is available.

In the "Questions" section below you will find questions that will help you to examine product demand using these analytical concepts.

QUESTIONS

1. Demand elasticity

- In analyzing product demand and demand sensitivity, which of the following have been considered:
  - ❏ price elasticity of demand
  - ❏ income elasticity of demand
  - ❏ cross price elasticity of demand?

- Has the audit team established elastic demand or inelastic demand?

Note: Figures 3a and 3b, Step 2 illustrate the effects of elastic demand and inelastic demand on total revenue.

2. Revenue concepts

- In establishing the relationship between sellers' revenues and the elasticity of demand, has the audit team defined the following:

❏ total revenue

❏ average revenue

❏ marginal revenue?

Note: Total revenue is the total amount spent by buyers for the product (TR = P + Q). Average revenue is the total outlay by buyers divided by the number of units sold, or the price of the product (AR = TR ÷ Q). Marginal revenue refers to the change in total revenue resulting from a change in sales volume.

3. Consumers' surplus

• When setting price, has consumers' surplus been assessed in terms of value-in-use and value-in-exchange?

4. Signals

• In order to convey quality information about the product or service to buyers, which information cues have been used:

❏ price of product

❏ brand or store name

❏ store decorations

❏ large expenditure on advertising?

Note: For these cues to serve as signals of quality, consumers must be able to discern differences in a product, service or firm characteristic across sellers and the quality of the product or service in the market must vary with this characteristic or attribute.

• Can the benefits of the product or service be conveyed by:

❏ search attributes

❏ experience attribute

❏ credence attribute?

Note: Exhibit 2, Step 2 provides definitions, examples and the effects of search, experience and credence attributes.

Having analyzed pricing decisions and assessed demand, the next step is to assess how customers form their perceptions of the value of products and recognize the important role that price plays in their perceptions. This is covered in detail in Step 3. A brief list of appropriate audit questions follows an outline of this step.

DETERMINE HOW YOUR BUYERS PERCEIVE PRICES

BACKGROUND

Price needs to be consistent with customers' perceived value of the product or service. In order to achieve this, it is important to understand how customers form their value perceptions. So when setting prices it is vital to look at four areas.

1. Perception.

2. Price, perceived quality and perceived value.

3. Major pricing errors.

4. Price thresholds.

In the "Questions" section below you will find a set of questions for assessing how your customers perceive prices and how this should affect price setting.

QUESTIONS

1. Perception

- When a product or service price is increased, is there adequate assessment of how significant this increase is to the customer?

- When comparing your product or service with that of your competitors, has the effect of the price difference been assessed as regards customer perception?

- Has the effect of information cues on this perceptual process by buyers been adequately assessed?

2. Price, perceived quality and perceived value

- Has there been adequate analysis of how product price influences the customers' perception of quality?

- Has there also been an assessment of the customers' perception of value?

Note: The role of price on the customer's perceptions of product quality, sacrifice, value, and willingness to buy is illustrated in Figure 4, Step 3. The figure also shows that customers may use external information cues as indicators of product quality.

3. Major pricing errors

- Has the new approach to pricing – value pricing – been implemented to increase sales?

Note: See "Price thresholds" below for further examples of pricing errors.

4. Price thresholds

- Has there been adequate analysis of price thresholds?

Note: The rule is that small, equally perceptible changes in a response correspond to proportional changes in the stimulus. So, if a product's price increase of $10 to $12 is sufficient to deter the customer, another product priced at $20 would have to be increased to $24 before affecting sales.

Note: Two pricing errors can be discussed in terms of price thresholds: not distinguishing between perceived value and price, and not distinguishing between absolute price and relative price.

Price thresholds need to be looked at in terms of:

❏ absolute price thresholds

❏ differential price thresholds

❏ effects of references prices on perceived value

❏ price and perceived value.

Absolute price thresholds

- Have the limits or absolute thresholds to the relationship between price, perceived quality and perceived value been established (ie both lower and upper price thresholds)?

Differential price thresholds

- Has the price setter determined the effect of perceived price difference between the company's products or services and that of its competitors on customers' choices?

- Specifically, have the customers' purchasing decisions been assessed in terms of:

    ❏ the relative price differences between competing brands

    ❏ different offerings in a product line

    ❏ price levels at different points in time?

Note: Behavioral price research has shown three important points regarding price elasticity.

1 In general, customers are more sensitive to perceived price increases than to perceived price decreases (ie it is easier to lose sales by increasing price than to gain sales by reducing price).

2 On occasions a product may provide a unique benefit which customers value and which makes it less price sensitive.

3 The frequency of past price changes can influence customers' sensitivity to price changes.

Effects of references prices on perceived value

- Has the customer's reference price been assessed in terms of the signal of product quality?

- If so, which of the following apply:

  ❏ the range of prices last paid

  ❏ the current market price

  ❏ the perceived average market price

  ❏ a belief about a fair price to pay

  ❏ an expected price to pay?

Note: A price needs to be compared to another price by customers. Not recognizing this leads to another pricing error: not distinguishing between pricing strategies and pricing tactics.

Price and perceived value

- Has there been a thorough assessment of how customers use price information to judge the value of the product and the influence this evaluation has on their purchase decision?

Having considered how its customers perceive prices, evaluated what its prices communicate to the customer about its products' quality and value and looked at the differences between perceived value and price, and between absolute and relative prices, the audit team now needs to examine the effect of cost on price setting. Step 4 provides the information on costs and cost analysis. A brief list of appropriate audit questions follows an outline of this step.

DETERMINE THE RELEVANT COSTS FOR THE PRICING STRATEGY

BACKGROUND INFORMATION

Analyzing cost data is useful when setting price, but it only indicates whether the product or service can be provided and sold profitably at any particular price and does not indicate how much markup or markdown on cost buyers will accept.

It is essential that costs for pricing are based on the future as current or past information is unlikely to provide an adequate basis for profit projections. Hence product costs must be based on the expected purchase costs of materials, labor, product development, advertising and promotion, distribution costs and additional expenses.

When looking at costs, four broad areas should be considered.

1. Cost concepts.

2. Break-even analysis.

3. Profit analysis.

4. Profit analysis for multiple products.

In the "Questions" section below you will find a set of questions to determine the relevant costs when considering your pricing strategy.

QUESTIONS

1. Cost concepts

- Has cost data been classified into its fixed and variable components in order to trace the effects of changes in price, volume, or product selling mix?

- Has cost data also been properly attributed to the activity causing the cost?

Note: The cost concepts of importance to pricing are outlined in Exhibit 3, Step 4 by activity (direct/traceable/attributable costs, indirect traceable costs and common costs) and by behavior (direct variable costs, semivariable costs and fixed costs).

- Has there been a thorough investigation into how costs are incurred and how they behave as activity levels alter?

2. Break-even analysis

- Have price setters used break-even analysis to calculate what quantity of product the company needs to sell just to cover costs?

- In order to complete the break-even analysis, have the following fixed costs been considered:
  - ❏ managers' salaries
  - ❏ building maintenance
  - ❏ insurance
  - ❏ mortgage payments or rent
  - ❏ debt service
  - ❏ others?

- In order to complete the break-even analysis, have the following variable costs been considered:
  - ❏ hourly wages
  - ❏ raw materials
  - ❏ transportation and shipping
  - ❏ sales commissions
  - ❏ others?

Note: The formula for break-even calculations is:

$$\text{Break-even (in units)} = \frac{\text{fixed costs}}{(\text{price} - \text{unit variable costs})}$$

3. Profit analysis

- Has a profit analysis of each product or service been completed in order to establish the best pricing strategy to follow?

Note: One of the most important pieces of data resulting from a profit analysis is the contribution ratio or profit–volume ratio (PV), as it is usually referred to. This is the percentage of sales dollars available to cover fixed costs and profits after deducting variable costs and is calculated as follows:

$$\text{Profit–volume ratio} = \frac{(\text{price} - \text{variable costs})}{\text{price}}$$

or

$$\frac{\$ \text{ contribution per unit}}{\text{price}}$$

4. Profit analysis for multiple products

- For multiproduct companies, has the emphasis correctly been placed on achieving the maximum amount of contribution revenue for each product instead of attempting to maximize sales revenues?

- Has the PV ratio been used to analyze the relative profit contribution of each product in the line?

Note: In multiproduct companies, the PV is determined by weighting the PV of each product by the percentage of the total dollar volume for all products in the line.

Having established and analyzed cost data and understood what determines profit, you will now need to determine the individual characteristics of each price decision. Extensive information for this is provided in Step 5. A brief list of appropriate audit questions follows an outline of this step.

DETERMINE THE CHARACTERISTICS OF EACH SPECIFIC PRICE DECISION

BACKGROUND INFORMATION

When considering price, a company needs to consider many factors including the type of customer to whom the product is to be sold, whether to offer volume discounts, discounts for early payment, discounts for cash, whether to set resale prices, the price relationships between multiple products, and whether to charge transportation costs.

In analyzing each price decision, there are five aspects to consider.

1. Pricing new products.

2. Pricing during growth.

3. Pricing during maturity.

4. Pricing a declining product.

5. Focused price reductions.

In the "Questions" section below you will find a set of questions to ensure that all factors are considered when making pricing decisions.

QUESTIONS

- Have pricing decisions been made taking the following into account?

  ❏ What to charge for the different products and services marketed by the firm.

  ❏ What to charge different types of customers.

  ❏ Whether to charge different types of distributors the same price.

  ❏ Whether to give discounts for cash and how quickly payment should be required to earn them.

  ❏ Whether to suggest resale prices or only set prices charged to·one's own customers.

  ❏ Whether to price all items in the product line as if they were separate or to price them as a 'team'.

  ❏ How many different price offerings to have of one item.

  ❏ Whether to base prices on the geographical location of buyers (i.e. whether to charge for transportation).

1. Pricing new products

- In pricing a new product, are you confident that the price is right and not too low or too high?

There are various aspects that need to be considered when looking at pricing new products including:

❏ factors to consider

❏ buyers' alternatives

❏ skimming pricing

❏ penetration pricing.

Factors to consider

- Has the price sensitivity of demand been taken into account?

- Have the seller's incremental promotional and production costs also been taken into account?

- Has the product's worth to the buyer rather than its cost to the seller been the controlling consideration?

- Has the relationship between the buyers' perceived benefits in the new product relative to the total acquisition costs and relative to the alternative products been assessed?

Buyers' alternatives

- Have competitive products or services been used to assess the price–performance package of a new product or service, thus establishing its relative attractiveness?

- In order to achieve this assessment, have the following steps been followed:

  ❏ determine the main uses for the new product

  ❏ for each main use, list the buyers' best alternatives

  ❏ for each main use, determine how well the new product's performance meets the customers' requirements compared with the alternatives

  ❏ forecast the prices of alternative products in terms of transaction prices (the net price after all discounts)

  ❏ estimate the superiority premium

❑ calculate a 'parity price' for the new product relative to the buyer's best alternative choice?

Note: Consumer definitions of price, quality and value-added performance characteristics are provided in Exhibit 5, Step 5.

There are two main alternatives when pricing a new product: 'skimming' pricing and 'penetration' pricing.

Skimming pricing

• Has a strategy of pricing high with large promotional expenditures during market introduction (skimming) been chosen?

• If so, which of the following reasons applies:

❑ sales are likely to be less sensitive to price in the early stages

❑ it is a device for breaking up the market

❑ it is safer given unknown elasticity of demand

❑ high prices may produce greater dollar sales volume during market development

❑ a capacity constraint exists

❑ there is a perceived value in the product by potential customers?

Note: Skimming is not always appropriate in these scenarios and can have drawbacks.

Penetration pricing

• Have low prices been used as a wedge to get into mass markets (penetration pricing) early on?

• If so, which of the following scenarios applies:

❑ potential buyers of the product are sensitive to price, even at its launch

❑ it is possible to achieve substantial reductions in unit costs by producing and selling large volumes

❑ soon after its introduction, the new product faces strong competition

❑ no section of buyers is prepared to pay a higher price for the product?

• Is it understood that low prices and low profit margins must be offset by high sales volumes?

- Has a combination of skimming and penetration been instigated ie adopting skimming pricing during a product's introduction and then once competitors have entered the market, they switch to penetration pricing?

- In choosing between skimming and penetration pricing for a new product, has consideration been given to the ease and speed with which competitors can bring out alternatives?

2. Pricing during growth

- When pricing products during the growth stage, have the following three essential points been considered:

  ❏ the range of feasible prices has narrowed since the introductory stage

  ❏ unit variable costs may have decreased due to the experience factor

  ❏ fixed expenses have increased because of increased capitalization and marketing costs?

- Will the price chosen, subject to competitive conditions, help to generate a sales dollar volume and thus achieve target profit contribution?

3. Pricing during maturity

- As a product moves into the maturity and saturation stages, have past pricing decisions been reviewed and a price change been considered?

- If a price reduction strategy has been adopted, have the following requirements all been satisfied:

  ❏ beginning with a relatively high PV ratio

  ❏ an opportunity for accelerating sales growth existing

  ❏ demand is price elastic?

4. Pricing a declining product

- During the declining phase of a product's life, is the company considering remaining in the market because is has both excess capacity and revenues still exceed all direct costs?

- Has consideration been given to raising the price of a declining product to increase the contribution per sales dollar?

5. Focused price reductions

- When considering a reduction in prices, which of the following two reasons applies:

  ❏ competitive pressures exist

  ❏ there are price-sensitive buyers in the market?

- Has information from conducting pricing research and marketing cost analyzes been available when developing a focused price reduction strategy?

Focused price reductions can be implemented in the following ways:

❏ base product versus option prices

❏ channel-specific pricing

❏ vary prices according to customers' perceived values

❏ product redesign

❏ price bundling.

Base product versus option prices

- Has consideration been given to selling just the basic product without any add-on features?

- If so, is the aim to appeal to:

  ❏ a price-sensitive market

  ❏ those who want only the basic product

  ❏ other buyers who are not price sensitive?

Channel-specific pricing

- Has a strategy of identifying distribution channels serving price-sensitive customers and offering lower-priced products only through these channels been adopted?

Vary prices according to customers' perceived values

- Has consideration been given to offering lower prices for demand occurring during off-peak hours, e.g. off-peak long distance phone calls?

Product redesign

- If the product were changed in some way and sold as a separate, lower-priced product, would it appeal to price-sensitive customers?

Price bundling

- Has consideration been given to offering two or more products or services at a price less than the sum of the individual prices?

The audit team should now have made all the fundamental pricing decisions, considered in depth how new products should be priced, and assessed the lifecycle stage of each product and the most appropriate pricing strategy. It is now necessary to bring together individual product pricing decisions into an overall multiple product pricing strategy. Key information for this is provided in Step 6. A brief list of appropriate audit questions follows an outline of this step.

INTEGRATE SPECIFIC PRICE DECISIONS INTO AN OVERALL PRICING STRATEGY

BACKGROUND INFORMATION

Due to the demand and cost interrelationships inherent within a multiple product company, and because there are usually several price segments, pricing multiple products is one of the main challenges facing a pricing manager. In particular, three pricing decisions are required: determining the lowest-priced product and its price; determining the highest-priced product and its price; and setting the price differentials for all intermediate products.

When looking at an overall pricing strategy, two concepts need to be looked at in detail:

1. Price bundling.
2. Yield management.

In the "Questions" section below you will find a set of questions to assist in establishing an overall pricing strategy.

QUESTIONS

1. Price bundling

• Have any products been bundled together at a special price?

Two important principles are involved in price bundling:

❑ rationale for price bundling
❑ mixed bundling.

Rationale for price bundling

• Can several products or services be offered together using the same facilities, equipment and personnel?

• If price bundled, are the incremental costs of selling additional units generally low relative to the company's total costs?

• Does price bundling fulfill the objective of stimulating demand for the company's product line to achieve cost savings for the whole operation while increasing net contributions to profits?

Mixed bundling

- Has consideration been given to mixed bundling where the buyer can either purchase products or services individually or as a package?

- Or has mixed-leader bundling (where the price of one product is discounted if the first product is purchased at full price) been considered?

- Alternatively, is mixed-joint bundling (a single price for the combined set of services) a possibility?

- If mixed bundling has been chosen, are the products selected for bundling relatively small in unbundled sales volume?

- If mixed-leader bundling is chosen, does the lead product fulfill the following requirements:
  - ❏ is price elastic
  - ❏ has attributes easy to evaluate before purchase
  - ❏ being the higher-volume product in the bundle
  - ❏ being the lower-margin product in the bundle?

- If mixed-joint bundling has been selected, do the following requirements apply:
  - ❏ the contribution margin for each product is about equal
  - ❏ the unbundled sales volumes are about equal
  - ❏ each product's demand is price elastic
  - ❏ each product complements the other products?

2. Yield management

- Is the segmentation pricing strategy of yield management as practiced by the airlines appropriate to your products or services?

Having made the essential pricing decisions regarding lowest-priced and highest-priced products and set price differentials for intermediate products, considered bundling products as a package, and decided whether yield management is applicable to your products or services, the final step is to look at developing an administrative structure for managing the pricing function. Extensive information for this is given in Step 7. A brief list of appropriate audit questions follows an outline of this step.

ASSESS THE ADMINISTRATIVE STRUCTURE FOR MANAGING THE PRICING FUNCTION

BACKGROUND INFORMATION

One of the most difficult parts of the pricing decision is developing procedures and policies for administering prices. It should be remembered that the list price is rarely the price actually paid by the buyer but instead is affected by discounts for volume or early payments, extending credit and charging for transportation. In addition, pricing decisions can have a considerable effect on dealers', distributors' and salespeoples' effort. Hence the importance of a carefully implemented and maintained company pricing policy.

When looking at administering a pricing policy, two aspects will be covered:

1. Developing a price structure.

2. An overview of discount decisions.

In the "Questions" section below you will find a set of questions to assist in assessing price administration.

QUESTIONS

1. Developing a price structure

- Which of the following price adjustment or price differentials scenarios dealt with by price administration apply to your company:

  ❏ sales made in different quantities

  ❏ sales made to different types of middlemen

  ❏ sales made to buyers in different geographic locations

  ❏ sales made with different credit or collection policies

  ❏ sales made at different times of the day, month, season or year?

- Has your price administration linked pricing strategy to overall marketing strategy and thus recognized price structure as a valuable part of a joint strategy?

- Have the key factors differentiating price-market segments been identified?

2. An overview of discount decisions

- Which of the six primary forms of discount are you utilizing:
    - ❏ trade
    - ❏ functional
    - ❏ quantity
    - ❏ cash
    - ❏ promotional
    - ❏ seasonal?

Note: The characteristics of the six major discounts are outlined in Exhibit 6, Step 7 while Exhibit 7, Step 7 calculates the discounts for a product qualifying for all types of price reduction.

CONCLUSION

All of the questions listed in this section will hopefully help you to plan an audit that will establish, implement and maintain your company's price strategy. The extensive explanations in Part 1 will help you to answer these questions to best effect.

Good luck!

Part 1: **Kent B. Monroe** *is the J.M. Jones Professor of Marketing and Head, Department of Business Administration, University of Illinois, Champaign-Urbana. He has pioneered research on the information value of price and authored the leading text* Pricing: Making Profitable Decisions, *2nd ed., McGraw-Hill, 1990. His research has been published in the* Journal of Marketing Research, Journal of Consumer Research, Journal of Marketing, Management Science, Journal of the Academy of Marketing Science, Journal of Retailing, Journal of Consumer Affairs *and the* Journal of Business Research. *Dr. Monroe has served as a consultant on pricing, marketing strategy, and marketing research, to business firms, governments, and the United Nations.*

Part 2 has been adapted from The Company AuditGuide *published by Cambridge Strategy Publications Ltd.* **Part 3** *has been developed by Cambridge Strategy Publications Ltd.*